CW00520307

Snakes of Australia

Graeme F. Gow

SNAKES OF AUSTRALIA

Angus&Robertson
An imprint of HarperCollins*Publishers*

To Stephen, Joanne and Lisa

An Angus & Robertson Publication

Angus&Robertson, an imprint of
HarperCollins*Publishers*
25 Ryde Road, Pymble, Sydney, NSW 2073, Australia
31 View Road, Glenfield, Auckland 10, New Zealand

First published in Australia by Angus & Robertson Publishers in 1976
Reprinted in 1980
This revised edition 1983
Reprinted in 1985, 1986, 1989, 1991, 1993

National Library of Australia
Cataloguing-in-Publication data:

Gow, Graeme F.
Snakes of Australia.

Rev. ed.
Previous ed.: Sydney: Angus & Robertson, 1976
Bibliography.

Includes index.
ISBN 0 207 14437 0.

1. Snakes — Australia — Identification. I. Title.

597.96'0994.

Cover photograph: Ingram's Brown Snake (Pseudonaja ingrami)
Printed in Hong Kong

12 11 10 9 8 7 6
97 96 95 94 93

Acknowledgements

I have enjoyed writing this book immensely, and if it assists the field man and the layman alike, then the effort has been more than worthwhile.

For assistance and advice during the preparation of the manuscript I am grateful to Dr H. Cogger, Curator of Reptiles at the Australian Museum, and to D. R. McPhee. I am especially grateful to Louis Robichaux and Joe Bredl for their encouragement and companionship on major expeditions spanning four states. To Steve Swanson, Paul Horner, John Cann, Phil Akers, Sylvie Smith, John McLoughlin, Bruce Morrison, John Edwards, Jim Wertz and George Cann, I am grateful not only for their capable assistance in the field but also for the many specimens collected on my behalf.

To the late and great George Cann, former Curator of Taronga Zoo's reptiles and founder of the La Perouse reptile exhibit, I am indebted for the inspiration he gave me personally and also countless other herpetologists.

Where acknowledged I am grateful to John Cann, P. Horner and G. Schmida for photographs. The remainder are the work of Steve Swanson to whom I owe especial thanks.

To Miss Margaret Boesenberg, who typed part of my manuscript, I also wish to express my thanks.

Also published by Angus and Robertson in this series

What Bird Is That?
Neville W. Cayley

Lizards Of Australia
Stephen Swanson

Tropical Fishes Of The Great Barrier Reef
Tom C. Marshall

Tortoises Of Australia
John Cann

Insects Of Australia
John Goode

Butterflies Of Australia
I. F. B. Common and D. F. Waterhouse

Contents

Introduction

The growing interest in herpetology and the many enquiries I constantly receive regarding Australian snakes have prompted me to prepare this book in an endeavour to assist the layman with the identification of all known species. For the beginner herpetologist I have tried to cover as simply as possible the basic rules of successfully and safely maintaining snakes in captivity. A great deal of research remains to be done, since the full habits of virtually all species are to date unknown.

All dedicated herpetologists genuinely interested in furthering our knowledge of Australian snakes can contribute greatly by co-operating with the appropriate museum in their home state. This is best accomplished by making available to them live or preserved specimens along with pertinent data (i.e. locality and captivity records), as they are always grateful to obtain this material.

There is still a great deal of confusion regarding the scientific names at present being used for certain species or groups of Australian snakes. An increasing amount of research is now being undertaken on the correct classification of these controversial groups. This, of course, will again bring about more changes, but the end result will mean a stable system to work from. Therefore, the scientific names used in this book comply only with those accepted by the majority of the world's leading herpetologists.

There are some 140 different kinds of land snake known to occur through all regions of Australia. Of this rather alarming total only a small number are dangerous to man; the majority are small species whose fangs and venoms are effective only against the small prey on which they feed.

There are 22 species of harmless blind snakes, TYPHLOPIDAE, found in Australia; they are all similar in appearance and habits. One typical member is illustrated, and there is a general description of the rather vague habits of this interesting group. A key to the Australian blind snakes is also reproduced.

There are currently 13 species of pythons, PYTHONINAE, found in Australia, ranging in size from Australia's largest snake, the scrub python, *Python amethistinus*, which inhabits northern Queensland and grows to a length of at least seven and a half metres, to the western children's python, *Liasis perthensis,* of Western Australia which rarely attains 60 centimetres in length.

The next group are known as colubrid snakes, COLUBRIDAE; this is in fact the largest and most widely distributed family of snakes in the world. Australia, however, has only 12 representatives of this group. This number is divided among three subfamilies, namely: COLUBRINAE, which contains four non-venomous land snakes; BOIGINAE, which contains one member only, the widely distributed brown tree snake, *Boiga irregularis*, a venomous back-fanged land snake not dangerous to man; and the HOMALOPSINAE, with six species, which are venomous back-fanged water snakes restricted to the tropical north Australian coast and are harmless to man. The ACROCHORDINAE is a small family containing two non-venomous aquatic snakes known as file snakes.

The next and largest Australian family are the elapids, ELAPIDAE; all members are front-fanged venomous land snakes. They range in size from the taipan, *Oxyuranus scutellatus*, one of the world's deadliest snakes and also the longest venomous snake in Australia (with a maximum length of almost three metres), to such small species as Krefft's dwarf snake, *Cacophis krefftii*, which grows to a known length of only 33 centimetres.

There are 32 species of sea snakes, HYDROPHIIDAE, recorded from Australian waters. An introductory chapter covering their general biology is given. Two are illustrated to show the diversity of this group. Treatment of sea snake envenomation is given in the relevant chapter on "The Treatment of Snake Bite".

General Habits

Feeding

Snakes prefer live food caught and killed by themselves; most species do, however, accept freshly killed food in captivity. Each snake has its particular food preferences, which, depending on the species, may include insects, frogs, fish, reptiles, birds and mammals. The prey is usually killed by constriction, the injection of venom, or simply grasped and eaten alive. Venomous species usually strike their prey only once and let go, knowing it will not go far before dying. Cold-blooded prey may be held longer, for the venom's action against this type of prey is slower. Certain venomous species, of which the common brown snake is a good example, also apply constriction to subdue prey.

The non-venomous species subdue their prey by two methods. Pythons strike their prey and, while holding it firmly in their strong jaws, throw several coils around it and commence squeezing immediately. The prey is not crushed to death as is commonly believed, but is held firmly, the constricting coils are increasingly tightened until the air supply has been cut off, and death from suffocation results. The Colubrine snakes strike and grasp their prey and, holding on tenaciously, commence swallowing immediately so that the victim may be eaten alive.

Snakes possess the remarkable ability to swallow prey much larger than the diameter of their own head and body. This feat is made possible by the elasticised ligament which joins the two halves of the lower jaw. The prey is nudged around until the head is located, most prey being eaten headfirst so that scales, fur or feathers offer little or no resistance. As the snake's jaws move over the head and onto the body they become dislocated, the upper and lower being moved forward independently. The sharp recurved teeth moving backwards and forwards enable the snake to draw itself over the prey. During this process the head undergoes enormous distension and the windpipe or glottis is projected forward to assist breathing. When this has been accomplished, the snake moves around yawning and stretching the jaws vigorously until the dislocated bones have been replaced and the head resumes its normal shape. By this time the food has been worked further down the body towards the stomach.

Sloughing

All snakes shed their skins at intervals; some species shed only once a year, others three or four times. Shedding is a more frequent occurrence with juvenile and young specimens, the process being greatly governed by a snake's rate of growth and state of health. Injured specimens also shed more frequently, until their wounds are completely healed. Healthy specimens usually shed the skin in one piece, with the exception of large pythons, which shed their skin in pieces. Approximately a week prior to sloughing the eyes become clouded and the skin lustreless, remaining like this for four to five days. The eyes then clear, and two or three days later the outer skin loosens and should be shed.

When about to shed the skin, a snake seeks out some projection to rub its head against. Working the skin loose at the lips, the snake gradually turns it backwards over the head and slowly crawls out, turning it inside out in the process. A close examination of the skin should reveal that the transparent protective scales which cover the eyes have also been shed.

Progression

In previous years it was thought that the ribs played the major role in a snake's progression, the theory then being that these acted as legs. It is now known that waves of muscle movements push the body forward in a series of curves, the ventral or belly scales gaining purchase from any irregularities on the ground. When a snake is placed on a smooth surface such as glass or linoleum, unable to exert any muscular thrust, it is virtually helpless.

Reproduction

Snakes produce their young by two methods; most of our non-venomous species are oviparous or egg-laying, while most of our venomous species are ovoviviparous or live-bearing. It must be mentioned, however, that there are exceptions in both cases. The oviparous snakes lay white elongate eggs, which have a parchment-like shell; these vary in size and number with the species. They are usually deposited amongst leaf mould, compost, in and under rotting logs and fallen timber; the site is carefully selected, for the eggs have to rely on natural moisture and heat for incubation. Pythons usually coil round their eggs to protect them and to aid in the incubation process.

Although the natural incubation period is not known, eggs of most species when hatched under artificial conditions have an incubation period that varies with temperature and usually ranges from ten to 14 weeks. The young emerge from the egg by means of an egg tooth located on the tip of the snout; this tooth is used to make slits in the egg from which the young can make their exit. The tooth is discarded along with the outer skin when the snake sheds for the first time.

The ovoviviparous or live-bearing species are also selective in choosing the area at which the birth is to take place. This may be amongst grass, tree-roots, fallen timber, secluded rock outcrops, or in and under rubbish and debris. These areas provide the newborn young with suitable cover and protection from their many predators. The young at birth may be contained in transparent sacs in which they can be seen struggling vigorously in an effort to break the membrane.

Whether oviparous or ovoviviparous they are completely independent of their parents from the moment of birth.

Fallacies

Snakes have been regarded since earliest times as fearsome, aggressive creatures, and unfortunately many fallacies, myths and superstitions still exist about them today. The mention of snakes will often create immense interest in any conversation; it usually becomes spiced with greatly exaggerated accounts of personal encounters with snakes resulting in their undeserved reputations and many misconceptions.

The following are corrections of the most common fallacies.

A snake's body is not slimy, but is quite dry to touch.

The forked tongue is a sensory organ and is not the fang or sting as is often believed.

The death adder cannot sting with its tail; the curved spine on the tip of the tail is only a soft modified scale.

Snakes show no preference for milk and, if given the choice, will drink water every time.

Snakes are not habitually aggressive and always prefer to retreat, attacking only if hurt or provoked.

The bandy bandy, although technically venomous, cannot inflict a serious bite and does not cause a fit for every ring on its body.

The bite of a carpet snake or any other reptile does not leave an annually recurring sore.

A snake's death will take place before or after sunset, depending on the extent of its injuries; the nerves, however, do remain active for some time after death.

Hoop snakes, the minute snake and snakes that crack themselves like whips exist only in the imagination.

Snakes have no external ears, are mainly insensitive to air-borne sounds and cannot be attracted or charmed by music.

Snakes cannot be rendered harmless by milking or by the removal of their fangs; the venom glands are equivalent to our own parotid or salivary glands, which simply means they are never completely dry, always retaining enough venom to cause a lethal bite, even after milking.

The fangs may be broken out, but the jagged butts remain, as do the reserve fangs, and are sufficient to cause a puncture or scratch, thus enabling venom to enter the bloodstream.

Fully formed young, which are occasionally found within freshly killed snakes, have not been swallowed for protection, but are simply in the oviducts awaiting birth.

The Symptoms and Treatment of Snake Bite

As snakes seldom attack unless provoked, the chances of a person being bitten in an unexpected encounter are remote, provided that common sense is used. If a snake is suddenly encountered, leave it alone; do not attempt to kill or catch it, for such acts of bravado often result in an unnecessary bite. Placing bare hands down rabbit burrows, under logs, rocks or sheets of iron lying on the ground is also asking for trouble, for these are all known haunts of snakes. When walking through areas in the bush that are densely populated with snakes, it is advisable to wear thick socks and boots.

Herpetologists who collect and keep venomous snakes as a hobby or for a living are more likely to be bitten than persons who only encounter snakes by chance.

In the event of a person being bitten it is of paramount importance to keep calm and not to panic, and at the same time to avoid any unnecessary movement. The victim should be reassured as convincingly as possible that death from snake bite is a rare occurrence. The bite from a venomous snake is purely a defensive measure and, depending on the circumstances, a lethal amount of venom may or may not be injected.

Symptoms of Snake Bite

The symptoms of snake bite vary greatly in every case. The initial sensation is similar to a pinprick but in some cases it is completely painless and the bite may go unnoticed.

A bite may consist of two distinct fang punctures, but sometimes single or multiple punctures (up to six) may be present. The fine, sharp fangs and teeth of Australian snakes often result in numerous fine scratches at the site of the bite, sometimes making the exact location of the fang punctures difficult to locate.

If significant envenoming has occurred, without first aid one would expect generalised symptoms like headache, vomiting, and so on, within 30 minutes.

As the venom starts to take effect, headache, nausea, vomiting, drowsiness and profuse sweating occur within one to two hours after the bite, the regional lymph nodes become markedly swollen, tender and painful (a definite indication of significant envenomation — Sutherland 1976). Severe abdominal and chest pains may also be present, diarrhoea is common — occasionally with bright blood. As the patient deteriorates the pupils dilate, double or blurred vision often occurs, speech becomes slurred, swallowing difficult and blood may be present in the urine.

Statistics show that the majority of victims reach hospital within two hours of the bite, but even if the victim happens to be in a remote area, death is very unlikely in less than eight hours, even without treatment.

First Aid for Snake Bite

The majority of bites occur on the lower limbs; bites to the head and body are, fortunately, very rare. Venom is usually deposited subcutaneously and spreads very rapidly.

Incision or excision of the bitten area is no longer recommended. Experiments have shown that these methods remove very little venom, and in many cases no venom has been injected. Cutting the bite can also be a traumatic experience for the victim, intensifying shock and thereby increasing the spread of venom through the circulation. The application of a tourniquet, for many years the first step recommended in the treatment of snake bite, has now become outdated.

Ideally, a broad constrictive bandage (a crepe bandage is best) should be applied to firmly cover the bitten area and as much of the limb as possible and the limb should then be immobilised by being placed in a sling or splint. As the spread and absorption of venom is partially via the lymphatics, the pressure of a constrictive bandage and the immobilisation of the limb assists greatly by reducing lymph production. A constrictive bandage and splint can also be tolerated comfortably, for some hours if necessary, without having to be released, another definite advantage over the tourniquet.

Immediate First Aid is as Follows:

1. Immediately apply a broad constrictive bandage covering the bitten area and as much of the limb as possible. If a bandage is unavailable, clothing can be torn into strips and effectively substituted. Bind as firmly as for a sprained ankle.
2. Do not *cut* or *wash* the bitten area.
3. Completely immobilise the affected limb by placing it in a sling or splint. Do not remove bandage or splint until the patient is given medical aid.
4. Reassure the victim that death from snake bite is rare; this is extremely important. Fear of death is unnecessary because effective antivenoms are available to counteract the bites of all species.
5. Do not allow the victim to drink alcohol.
6. Bring transport to the victim and proceed as quickly as possible to the nearest hospital. If possible, telephone the hospital giving relevant details and estimated time of arrival.
7. Inform the doctor in charge if the victim suffers from asthma, any form of allergy, or has previously received antivenom. This is to allow the doctor to prepare for the possibility of a serum reaction.
8. If the snake has been killed, take the specimen in for positive identification. This is not absolutely necessary since the poly-

valent antivenom currently being used neutralises the venom of all dangerous species (see C.S.L. Table 2). Treatment, however, is greatly simplified if the identity of the snake is known because a monovalent antivenom (antivenom for a specific species) should always be used in preference to polyvalent antivenom (see C.S.L. Table 1).

The following drawings demonstrate the method for the **lower limb**.

1. Apply a broad pressure bandage over the bite site as soon as possible (don't take off jeans as the movement of doing so will assist venom to enter the blood stream. Keep the bitten leg still!).
2. The bandage should be as tight as you would apply to a strained ankle.
3. Extend the bandages as high as possible.
4. Apply a splint to the leg.
5. Bind it firmly to as much of the leg as possible.

If the bandages and splint have been applied correctly, they will be comfortable and may be left on for several hours.

They should not be taken off until the patient has reached medical care.

The doctor will decide when to remove the bandages.

If venom has been injected it will move into the blood stream very quickly when the bandages are removed and the doctor should leave it in position until he or she has assembled appropriate antivenom and drugs which **may** have to be used when the dressings and splint are removed.

6. **Bites on hand or forearm.**

(A) Bind to elbow with bandages.
(B) Use splint to elbow.
(C) Use sling.

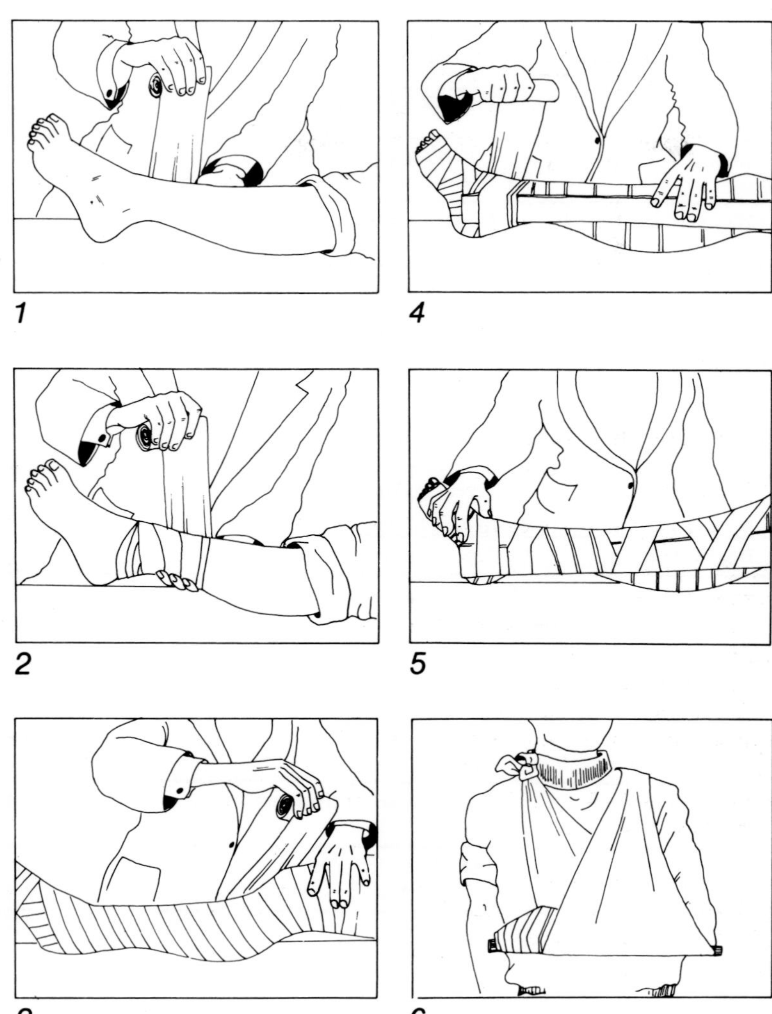
1
4
2
5
3
6

C.S.L. TABLE 1
ANTIVENOM DOSAGE WHEN SNAKE HAS BEEN POSITIVELY IDENTIFIED

SPECIES	*APPROPRIATE ANTIVENOM, INITIAL DOSE (Adults and Children)*	
Western Taipan or Small-scaled Snake	Taipan Antivenom	12,000 units
Taipan	Taipan Antivenom	12,000 units
Mainland Tiger Snake	Tiger Snake Antivenom	3000 units
Tasmanian Tiger Snake	Tiger Snake Antivenom	6000 units
Chappell Island Tiger Snake	Tiger Snake Antivenom	12,000 units
Other members of the genus *Notechis*	Tiger Snake Antivenom	3000 units
Copperhead	Tiger Snake Antivenom	3000–6000 units
Death Adder	Death Adder Antivenom	6000 units
Common Brown Snake and other members of the genus *Pseudonaja*	Brown Snake Antivenom	1000 units (2 ampoules)
King Brown Snake	Black Snake Antivenom	18,000 units
Papuan Black Snake	Black Snake Antivenom	18,000 units
Other members of the genus *Pseudechis*	Black Snake Antivenom or Tiger Snake Antivenom	6000 units 3000 units
Rough-scaled or Clarence River Snake	Tiger Snake Antivenom	3000 units
Australian Sea Snakes	*Enhydrina schistosa* Antivenom or Tiger Snake Antivenom	1000 units 12,000 units

C.S.L. TABLE 2
ANTIVENOM DOSAGE FOR AN UNIDENTIFIED SNAKE (ADULTS AND CHILDREN)

STATE	*APPROPRIATE ANTIVENOM, INITIAL DOSE*	
TASMANIA	Tiger Snake Antivenom	6000 units
VICTORIA	Tiger Snake Antivenom and Brown Snake Antivenom	3000 units 1000 units (2 ampoules)
NEW SOUTH WALES QUEENSLAND SOUTH AUSTRALIA WESTERN AUSTRALIA NORTHERN TERRITORY	POLYVALENT ANTIVENOM	Contents of one container
PAPUA NEW GUINEA	POLYVALENT ANTIVENOM	Contents of one container

The Care of Snakes in Captivity

In order to maintain a collection of healthy specimens, the following requirements are essential.

1. *Adequate housing:* the quarters must be well ventilated, escape-proof and cleaned regularly.
2. *Temperature:* a correct temperature of between 23 and 29 degrees Celsius; snakes are far easier to maintain when kept warm.
3. *Diet:* a stable diet and a regular supply of clean water must be provided.
4. *Health:* immediate treatment of injuries, illnesses and infestations is important.

Housing

Packing cases or sturdy boxes are easily converted to snake cages by the insertion of a sliding glass front and ventilation holes. Ordinary window glass is sufficient for housing small snakes, but six-millimetre plate should be used to house large or potentially dangerous specimens. The cage must be free of rough surfaces, it should be well ventilated and provide good visibility and easy access for safety, feeding and cleaning purposes. Wire fronts should not be used because snakes tend to rub their noses raw against them; this usually results in a severe and sometimes fatal infection. The most suitable covering for ventilation areas or holes is fine fibreglass mesh, of the type used in insect screens. Glass aquariums provided with tight-fitting lids such as pegboard are excellent quarters. These are popular with herpetologists because they are readily obtainable in various sizes, and when properly set up display specimens to their best advantage; they are also easy to maintain.

Setting up the Cage

The natural cage set-up is the most popular and attractive means of exhibiting specimens. This set-up may be varied to meet a particular species' requirements by the gathering of natural materials found in the bush. Ideal floor materials are soil, fine sand, gravel or dry leaves. Wood shavings, coarse sand or peat moss are not advisable in that they may adhere to food and, if swallowed, may result in damage to the stomach-wall causing intestinal irritations and sometimes death. The further addition of plants, ferns, cacti or artificial foliage adds greatly to a cage's decor. Virtually all species like a place of retreat and this can be provided in the form of bark, rocks, hollow limbs or logs which they can crawl in or under. For climbing species, such as pythons and tree snakes, a carefully selected branch should be provided, although it is not absolutely necessary. A rough stone or rock too large to be moved is a valuable asset since specimens need some such object to rub against and loosen the skin prior to shedding. When selecting a suitable water container, it must be remembered that snakes require water for both drinking and bathing; some species will soak themselves for long periods before sloughing. For small snakes the container should be shallow, otherwise they will not find the water. The water container should be placed in the cage so that it cannot be moved, for continually slopped water creates dampness, a condition detrimental to snakes.

Correct Temperature

The cheapest method of providing sufficient warmth is by installing an electric light bulb in the cage and by experimenting with bulbs of different wattage until one is found that maintains the cage temperature between 23 and 29 degrees Celsius. A thermometer should be placed in the cage and checked occasionally to ensure that the temperature is neither too high nor too low. This is best accomplished by fitting a thermostatic control. To graduate to a large and varied collection of snakes involves the building of a reptile house; however, the cost of erecting and heating a reptile house is very great and out of reach of the average herpetologist. Snakes kept in outside enclosures during the winter months become inactive and refuse food; during this period no attempt should be made to feed them, for in cold weather digestion is much slower, the food ferments and the specimen may die from food poisoning. In summer months when temperatures are high a shaded area should always be provided, for all snakes are easily killed by overexposure to the sun.

Food

Since most species prefer live food, a constant food supply is always a major problem. For this reason special care should be taken to limit your collection to the number of specimens that you can house and feed properly. Mice and rats can be bred, trapped, or purchased from pet shops. Sparrows are easily caught by means of a trap or net, and day-old chickens are readily obtainable from hatcheries. Cold-blooded prey, such as frogs, skinks and geckoes, must be caught by hand in the field. When an abundance of food is available, any excess mice, rats, birds, frogs, fish, lizards and snakes should be killed, frozen immediately and placed in the kitchen refrigerator. Failing a sympathetic family attitude, you may have to purchase a secondhand refrigerator. When storing the food, it should be wrapped in separate parcels so that it may be removed in portions as required. Most species will learn in captivity to take freshly killed or thawed food; this is the safest method of feeding. When leaving mice or rats in the cage, care should be taken that they are provided with food. Snakes that are sluggish or off their food are reluctant to defend themselves against hungry mice and rats, and the end result is a severely mutilated or dead snake. Snakes need to be fed once a week and should not be allowed to gorge themselves at every meal. It does not hurt to miss several feeds when food is scarce, provided the snakes are in good condition. Snakes in poor condition may be gradually conditioned by adding vitamins to their food. Cod-liver oil is excellent and can be injected into the food with a syringe, or alternatively a vitamin mineral supplement in capsule form may be inserted into the food.

Force Feeding

By this method food is forced by means of forceps, rod or some other suitable object down the throat of a snake and gently massaged by hand down the body and into the stomach. Normal foods can be used, although strips of meat or fish are easier to work with. Force feeding is a tricky operation at any time, and great care must be taken to avoid damaging fangs, teeth or the delicate walls of the oesophagus. The best and safest method is what is known as passive hand feeding. This involves the use of a syringe or plunger gun of some sort, attached to which is a length of rubber, plastic or glass tubing about 25 centimetres long and of a diameter to suit the size of the snake's mouth. A mixture is then prepared from finely ground meat, one egg, a teaspoon of cod-liver oil and a few drops of multivitamin mixture. Fill the syringe or gun with the mixture, attach the tube and slowly insert it into the snake's mouth and down the throat. When this has been done, the desired amount may be injected and the tube withdrawn slowly.

Diseases and Parasites

The two most common problems associated with keeping snakes in captivity are mites and mouth rot or canker.

Mites

When purchasing or exchanging snakes, they should first be carefully inspected for the presence of mites. These are minute crab-like blood-sucking parasites mostly apparent about the eyes or under the scales of the chin and neck. Heavily infested specimens are more easily detected by the presence of numerous white specks between and on the surface of the body scales; these are mite droppings. Mites multiply extremely rapidly and, if not immediately checked, will overpower snakes and cause their death. In previous years several methods were used to combat mites; the most common treatment was to soak specimens in water to remove any surface mites and then generously rub olive oil into the skin to suffocate those beneath the scales. This treatment had only mixed success and was a dangerous operation, especially with some of the larger venomous species. There is now a white powder called Neguvon, which, when dissolved in water and applied by spraying, is most effective in controlling mites. A teaspoon of Neguvon to half a litre of water gives the required strength, although this may be decreased or increased if necessary. The snakes should be sprayed liberally and then placed in a clean dry bag. This treatment should be repeated 48 hours later to eradicate any mite eggs missed in the first spraying. Since the solution is toxic, care should be taken that specimens do not swallow or drink the spray. The cage contents should be removed and placed in boiling water and disinfectant and then thoroughly cleaned. Wooden cages with cracks and corners should be treated to two applications of Neguvon, making sure at each spraying that any possible hiding places for mites are saturated. In the case of specimens kept in glass aquariums the quarters may be scrubbed out with hot water and strong disinfectant. New additions to the collection should be examined for mites before being liberated; if mites are found to be present, the specimen should be quarantined and treated accordingly. Neguvon is available from Bayer Australia Ltd, 47-67 Wilson Street, Botany, New South Wales.

Shelltox Pest Strips are readily available through a host of retailers and are used mainly in large collections or reptile houses to prevent the spread of mites. Although some keepers also cut these into small pieces so that they suit individual cages, care must be taken to ensure the pieces used are not overly large. The toxic fumes given off will not only overpower mites but also their host.

Mouth Rot or Canker

Mouth rot or canker is more commonly encountered among members of the python family, although it is not restricted to this group. It is believed that it starts from a minor mouth abrasion which becomes infected. This infection, if not checked in its infancy, produces a white scum-like substance which attacks gum tissue, loosening the teeth and affecting the bones of the jaw. In its final stages this matter prevents complete closure of the mouth, the glottis and the nasal passages become affected and breathing is greatly restricted. Specimens in this condition are best humanely destroyed. If detected and treated in its early stages, this disease may be cured by using an aqueous solution of sulphamezathine obtainable at chemists and sometimes sold under the name of Sul-Met. The mouth should be cleaned thoroughly, using a cotton swab to remove any loose canker; if probing is necessary, care should be taken to avoid bleeding. This solution should be applied with a medicine dropper or cotton swab one to three times daily to all affected surfaces of the mouth; the treatment should be continued until the condition clears. I have found, through experimentation, that Terramycin Poultry Formula is excellent in controlling this disease. This is a soluble powder, and half a teaspoon to a cup of water is the normal strength used. This solution is best administered by means of a syringe; the mouth is held open and the contents of the syringe squirted forcibly on all surfaces of the mouth. This treatment should be repeated one to three times daily until the infection has been completely arrested. This disease is not transferable to humans although it is contagious to other snakes; affected specimens should be isolated until cured. Visitors to the collection should be restrained from their favourite pastime of tapping on the glass in an effort to disturb specimens and make them strike; specimens provoked into striking against the glass easily injure themselves. It is always well to remember that a broken fang or tooth or oral and nasal abrasions may eventually lead to canker.

Terramycin Poultry Formula is a product of Pfizer Laboratories, Wharf Road, Ryde, New South Wales. This preparation is available only on prescription through veterinary wholesalers and is not available direct from the manufacturers.

Body Blisters

These soft blisters occasionally appear on the skin of snakes. Although their exact cause is as yet unknown, they are believed to be associated with damp conditions. If specimens suffering from this condition are not treated promptly, the blisters multiply rapidly and often prove fatal. The blisters should be opened and swabbed out with a good antiseptic, or alternatively opened and the snake placed in a bath of Terramycin solution. A well-covered aquarium or some escape-proof water container is filled to a depth of eight centimetres and enough Terramycin Poultry Formula added to colour the water. Two to three soakings of approximately two hours' duration have good results. Damp conditions should, of course, be completely eliminated.

Colds and Pneumonia

Colds and pneumonia in snakes are easily detected by the following symptoms. The forked tips of the tongue stick together and the throat becomes distended with fluid which is sometimes emitted in the form of bubbles from the mouth and nostrils. Specimens with bad congestion are constantly wheezing and opening their mouths as they experience extreme breathing difficulties. Specimens kept in cold, damp environments are particularly prone to colds and pneumonia, and even specimens kept under ideal conditions sometimes unaccountably contract these diseases. Although there is no effective cure, the best results have been obtained with sulphadiazine tablets and nasal drops. Affected specimens should be given two tablets per week and treated to a daily dose of nasal drops to ease congestion.

Open Wounds

Cuts or other such wounds should be treated as soon as practicable with an appropriate healing ointment or an antibiotic powder such as Neosporin, which I have found most effective in healing wounds of this nature. Neosporin tropical antibiotic powder is distributed by Burroughs Wellcome and Company, and is obtainable on prescription from your local chemist.

Identification

Scale Counting

Since the colour and form of a particular species of snake may vary throughout the extent of its distribution, a more satisfactory method of identification than general appearance is necessary. The most accurate and widely accepted procedure is to examine and record the scalation arrangement. The first step is to count the mid-body scales: that is, a single row of scales around the body, excluding the ventral scale. All of the ventral scales are then counted from the neck to the anal covering. Next it is necessary to determine whether the anal covering is single or divided. Below the anal covering are the subcaudals, which may be single, divided or a combination of both. They are counted in the same manner as the ventrals, a divided pair registers one count.

The illustration overleaf will assist in outlining the scale-counting procedure.

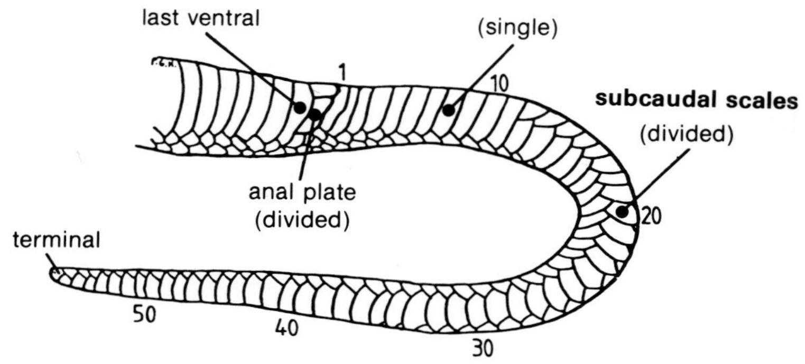

Dorsal Scales

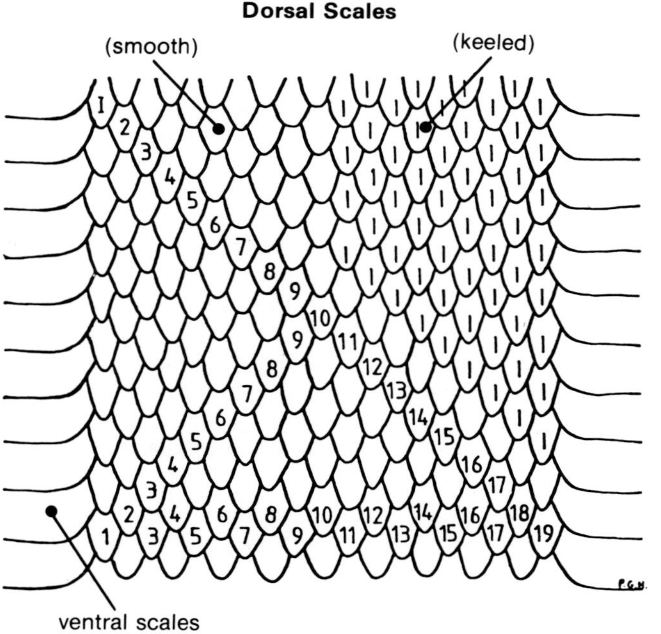

Snakes of Australia

FAMILY TYPHLOPIDAE (Blind Snakes)

GENUS *RAMPHOTYPHLOPS*
Fitzinger, 1843

Plate 1

RANGE: There are 22 species widely distributed throughout Australia with the exception of Tasmania.

IDENTIFICATION: These snakes have worm-like bodies and are, in fact, often mistaken for large earthworms. They may be identified, however, by their smooth scales around the entire body, lacking the broad ventral or belly scales of other snakes. They have minute eyes, which in appearance resemble two indistinct dots. The tail is short and blunt and terminates in a small spine which serves as an aid in progression. The colour varies through the species, but is usually pinkish-brown, grey-brown or black above and pinkish-white below.

REMARKS: Blind snakes are usually found in soft earth beneath large rocks, stumps, in or under rotten logs, in termite mounds and are often discovered when dug out of gardens. They are nocturnal in habit, venturing above the ground on warm nights and especially after rain, which seems to increase their activity. Reproductive data is scanty; however, I have recorded one clutch of 5 elongate eggs from a specimen of *Ramphotyphlops australis* collected at Renmark, South

Australia. The food consists of termites, worms, ants and their eggs. Blind snakes are non-venomous and are completely harmless. When first handled they emit a foul-smelling odour which remains on the hands for some time, despite frequent washings. This odour is believed to serve two purposes: as a means of defence and as a means for the sexes to locate each other during the mating season.

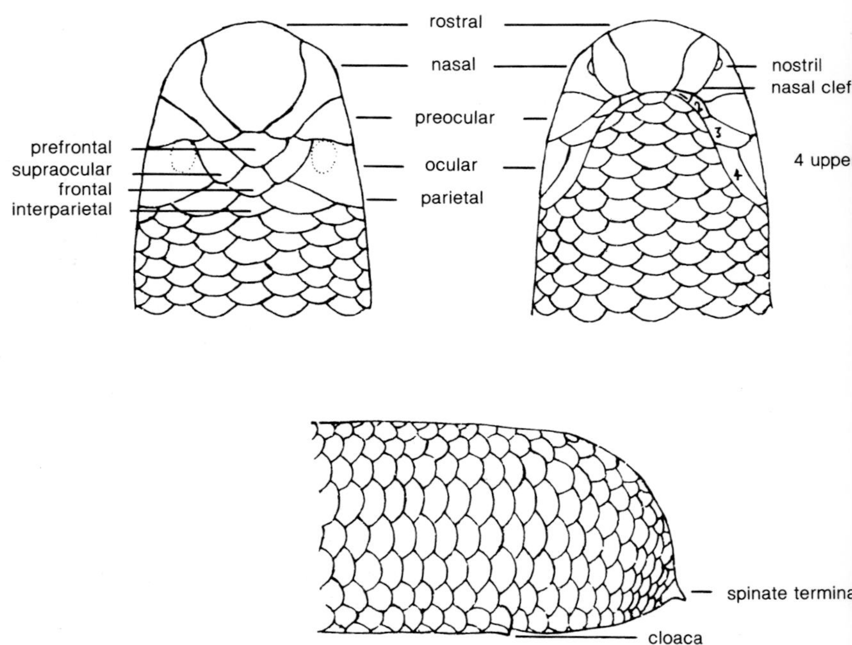

SCALATION TERMINOLOGY OF BLIND SNAKE (after Waite)

Key to the Australian *Ramphotyphlops*

1 a. Nasal cleft joining the first supralabial ... see 2
b. Nasal cleft joining the second supralabial ... see 5
c. Nasal cleft joining the preocular ... see 14

2 a. Mid-body scales in less than 24 rows ... see 3
b. Mid-body scales in 24 rows ... see 4

3 a. Mid-body scales in 18 rows ... *R. grypa*
b. Mid-body scales in 20 rows ... *R. proxima*
c. Mid-body scales in 22 rows ... *R. nigrescens*

4 a. Rostral slightly longer than broad, snout bluntly trilobed from above ... *R. unguirostris*
b. Rostral slightly longer than broad, snout rounded from above ... *R. yirrikalae*
c. Rostral extremely narrow, much longer than broad ... *R. ligata*

5 a. Mid-body scales in 16 rows ... see 6
b. Mid-body scales in 18 rows ... see 7
c. Mid-body scales in 20 rows ... see 9
d. Mid-body scales in 22 rows ... see 13

6 a. Nasal cleft completely divides nasal scale ... *R. leptosoma*
b. Nasal cleft does not completely divide nasal scale ... *R. minima*

7 a. Nasal cleft completely divides nasal scale ... see 8
b. Nasal cleft does not completely divide nasal scale ... *R. guentheri*

8 a. Snout bluntly pointed in profile ... *R. affinis*
b. Snout hooked in profile ... *R. nigroterminata*

9 a. Nasal cleft completely divides nasal scale ... *R. broomi*
b. Nasal cleft does not completely divide nasal scale ... see 10

10 a. Nasal cleft not visible from above ... see 11
b. Nasal cleft visible from above ... *R. wiedii*

11 a. No distinct whitish glands, visible between head shields ... see 12

b.	Distinct whitish glands, visible between head shields	*R. leucoprocta*
12 a.	Snout rounded from above	*R. pinguis*
b.	Snout trilobed from above	*R. bituberculata*
13 a.	Nasal cleft visible from above	*R. polygrammica*
b.	Nasal cleft not visible from above	*R. australis*
14 a.	Mid-body scales in 20 rows	see 15
b.	Mid-body scales in 22 rows	*R. endotera*
15 a.	Nasal cleft does not completely divide nasal scale	see 16
b.	Nasal cleft completely divides nasal scale	*R. bramina*
16 a.	Body uniform in coloration	*R. diversa*
b.	Body with a series of longitudinal streaks	*R. tovelli*

FAMILY BOIDAE

SUBFAMILY PYTHONINAE

(Pythons)

GENUS *ASPIDITES*

Black-headed Python **Plate 1**

Aspidites melanocephalus (Krefft, 1864)

RANGE: Northern Australia, extending into the drier inland areas.

IDENTIFICATION: Head slightly pointed, indistinct from neck; robust body. Dorsal coloration is light to dark brown with numerous narrow, dark cross-bands on the body and tail. The head, neck and throat are glossy black. Ventral surface is creamish, usually with dark blotches. Juveniles, although replicas of the adults, are more vividly marked, being creamish with orange to brick-red bands.

Mid-body scales are in 50 to 65 rows; ventrals number 315 to 359; subcaudals are mostly single, numbering 60 to 75; anal scale is single.

Maximum length is about three metres.

REMARKS: A terrestrial nocturnal species which may be found in a wide variety of habitats. Although normally nocturnal, it may be found active on cool days, particularly during or after rain storms. It is an egg-layer and may produce about 10 eggs in a clutch; hatchlings are about 510 mm in length. It preys upon small mammals, birds and reptiles, including venomous snakes. Normally inoffensive, it can look quite threatening however, when employing its defensive display of elevating the head and forebody and hissing loudly.

Woma **Plate 2**

Aspidites ramsayi (Macleay, 1882)

RANGE: Arid desert areas of all states, except Victoria.

IDENTIFICATION: Head slightly pointed, indistinct from neck; robust body. Dorsal coloration is olive, brown or reddish-brown with numerous dark cross-bands on the body and tail. Ventral surface is cream to yellow, blotched with pink or brown.

Mid-body scales are in 50 to 65 rows; ventrals number 280 to 315; subcaudals are mostly single, numbering 40 to 55; anal scale is single.

Maximum length is about three metres.

REMARKS: This species, due to its remote habitat, is seldom collected and little is known of its biology. Although normally nocturnal and terrestrial, it is a competent climber when foraging for prey. It is an efficient hunter and prey rarely escapes the grip of its powerful jaws. It feeds upon small mammals, birds and reptiles. Inoffensive by nature, it shows little or no aggression, even when molested.

GENUS *CHONDROPYTHON*

Green Python **Plate 3**

Chondropython viridis (Schlegel, 1872)

RANGE: Northern Cape York Peninsula. Also found in New Guinea.

IDENTIFICATION: Large head distinct from the neck; stout, slightly compressed body, prehensile tail. Dorsal coloration in adults is any shade of emerald-green, with scattered white scales and white or bluish vertebral markings, often extending the length of the body. Ventral surface is creamish to bright yellow. Juveniles differ markedly from adults and may be either golden yellow, orange, brick-red or chocolate-brown, with a series of white oval markings on the sides and vertebral line.

Mid-body scales are in 50 to 75 rows; ventrals number 225 to 260; subcaudals are single, numbering 90 to 110; anal scale is single.

Maximum length is about two metres.

REMARKS: A nocturnal arboreal python which spends most of its life high in trees, shrubs or bamboo thickets where its coloration acts as an effective camouflage. It is an egg-layer and may produce up to 20 eggs in a clutch. It feeds upon small birds and mammals and it is interesting to note that captive juveniles have been recorded using their tails as a lure to attract prey.

GENUS *LIASIS*

Children's Python — Plate 4

Liasis childreni Gray, 1842

RANGE: Most common in Queensland, Northern Territory and Western Australia, but also occurs in northern parts of South Australia and north-western New South Wales.

IDENTIFICATION: Head distinct from the neck; robust body. Dorsal coloration varies through all shades of brown, with dark brown to black variegated markings, these often resembling cross-bands. Ventral surface is white to cream. In the Northern Territory and Western Australia unmarked specimens occur and this form warrants further investigation.

Mid-body scales are in 37 to 49 rows; ventrals number 255 to 300; subcaudals are mostly divided, numbering 30 to 45; anal scale is single.

Maximum length is about 1.5 metres.

REMARKS: Occurring through a wide variety of habitats, this is a nocturnal terrestrial species which, however, will not hesitate to climb if in pursuit of prey. It feeds upon small mammals, birds and reptiles, is an egg-layer and may produce about 15 eggs in a clutch. Newly hatched young may measure about 250 mm in length. As in most pythons, the female coils about the eggs to aid in incubation and to defend them from predators.

Water Python **Plate 4**

Liasis mackloti Duméril & Bibron, 1844

RANGE: Coastal northern Australia, from north-eastern Queensland, through the Northern Territory to the Kimberleys of Western Australia.

IDENTIFICATION: Head distinct from the neck; robust body. Dorsal coloration is iridescent dark olive-green or olive-brown. Ventral surface is yellow or apricot, excepting the undersurface of the tail which is dark brown.

Mid-body scales are in 40 to 55 rows; ventrals number 270 to 300; subcaudals are divided, numbering 60 to 80; anal scale is single.

Maximum length is about three metres.

REMARKS: As implied by its common name, this beautiful nocturnal python is normally found in close proximity to permanent water. It will not hesitate to take to the water if disturbed and is often observed in reed beds where it preys upon water birds and their eggs. An efficient and relentless hunter, it also consumes small mammals and reptiles, including juvenile crocodiles. It produces up to 22 eggs in a clutch and newly hatched young measure about 440 mm in length.

Olive Python **Plate 5**

Liasis olivaceus Gray, 1842

RANGE: Far northern Australia, from the Pilbara region of Western Australia, through the top of the Northern Territory to north-western Queensland.

IDENTIFICATION: Head distinct from the neck; robust body. Dorsal coloration is fawn to dark olive-brown. Ventral surface is white or cream.

Mid-body scales are in 58 to 72 rows; ventrals number 321 to 411; subcaudals are divided, numbering 90 to 119; anal scale is single.

Maximum length is in excess of 3.7 metres.

REMARKS: This large nocturnal species prefers rocky habitats such as ranges and gorges, particularly those bordering water courses. Little is known of its clutch sizes; Christian records one clutch of 11 eggs, their incubation period was 71 days and the largest hatchling measured 375 mm. It feeds upon small mammals, birds and reptiles.

SUBSPECIES: *Liasis olivaceus barroni* (Smith, 1981)
Distinguished from *L. o. olivaceus* by having less mid-body scale rows (58 to 63 versus 61 to 72) and more ventrals (374 to 411 versus 355 to 377). Only found in the Pilbara region of Western Australia, where specimens up to 5.5 metres in length have been reported.

Liasis olivaceus olivaceus (Gray, 1842)
Found through rest of species range.

Western Children's Python
Liasis perthensis Stull, 1932

RANGE: Pilbara region of Western Australia.

IDENTIFICATION: Head distinct from the neck; robust body. Dorsal coloration is light brown or brownish-grey, with darker variegated markings. Ventral surface is whitish.

Mid-body scales are in 31 to 35 rows; ventrals number 205 to 255; subcaudals are mostly divided, numbering 30 to 45; anal scale is single.

Maximum length is about 600 mm.

REMARKS: A small nocturnal species whose full habits are virtually unknown. The late Mr F. J. Mitchell collected seven specimens from within large termite mounds; also within the mounds were colonies of the gecko *Gehyra pilbara,* which is presumably the major prey item of this python.

GENUS *PYTHON*

Scrub Python **Plate 5**
Python amethistinus (Schneider, 1801)

RANGE: North-eastern Queensland, from Cape York Peninsula, south to about Townsville.

IDENTIFICATION: Head distinct from neck; slim elongate body; prehensile tail. Dorsal coloration is variable, being fawn to olive-brown, with numerous dark brown to black variegated zig-zag markings. Ventral surface is white or cream. Specimens from open forest are much lighter in coloration than those from dense rainforest.

Mid-body scales are in 35 to 50 rows; ventrals number 270 to 340; subcaudals are mostly divided, numbering 80 to 120; anal scale is single.

Maximum length is about 7.6 metres.

REMARKS: This slender arboreal species is Australia's longest snake; it inhabits open forest, rainforest and mangrove swamps. Although normally nocturnal, it is often observed basking in sun-lit rainforest clearings. It preys upon birds and mammals, including such large creatures as agile wallabies *Macropus agilis*. About 20 eggs may be laid in a clutch and the newly hatched young measure about 600 mm in length.

Centralian Carpet Python **Plate 6**
Python bredli Gow, 1981

RANGE: Central Australia.

IDENTIFICATION: Large head distinct from the neck; robust body; prehensile tail. Dorsal coloration is variable, being reddish to dark brown with numerous irregular, pale fawn to yellow dark-edged blotches, stripes and bars. This patterning is most prominent posteriorly. Ventral surface is creamy white, with the posterior ventral scales irregularly edged with black.

Mid-body scales are in 52 to 54 rows; ventrals number 283 to 295; subcaudals are mostly divided, numbering 82 to 92; anal scale is single.

Maximum length is about 2.6 metres.

REMARKS: An arboreal nocturnal species which inhabits the rocky ranges of central Australia. It is an egg-layer and may produce up to 40 eggs in a clutch; females coil about the eggs to aid in the incubation and to protect them. Hatchlings measure about 300 mm and weigh about 15 grams. An efficient hunter, it preys upon mammals and birds which it subdues with constriction.

Oenpelli Python **Plate 7**
Python oenpelliensis Gow, 1977

RANGE: Known only from the western Arnhem Land escarpment, Northern Territory.

IDENTIFICATION: Head distinct from the neck; slim elongate body; long prehensile tail. Dorsal coloration is pale fawn, merging to light putty-grey on the lower sides. A series of dark grey or brown blotches and streaks are arranged in four or five longitudinal rows. This patterning becomes more obscure posteriorly. Scales on the tail are dark-edged, producing a reticulated effect. Ventral surface is off-white to pale yellow.

Mid-body scales are in 69 to 70 rows; ventrals number 429 to 455; subcaudals are mostly divided, numbering 145 to 163; anal scale is single.

Maximum length is about five metres.

REMARKS: A nocturnal arboreal species which inhabits the rugged sandstone escarpment of western Arnhem Land. Virtually nothing is known of the habits of this rare python; most specimens have been found secreted in or amongst the sandstone scree-slope rubble and crevices, but it has also been found in tree tops, out on the surrounding flood plain. If feeds upon mammals and birds.

Diamond and Carpet Pythons **Plates 7, 8**
Python spilotus (Lacépède, 1804)

RANGE: From the Kimberleys of Western Australia, through the "Top End" of the Northern Territory, most of Queensland and New South Wales, along the Murray River to southern South Australia and south-western Western Australia.

IDENTIFICATION: This species is split into two colour morphs encompassing three subspecies: the Diamond

Python *P. s. spilotus* and the Carpet Pythons, *P. s. variegatus* and *P. s. imbricatus*. They are all similar in body form, having large heads distinct from the neck, robust bodies and prehensile tails. The dorsal coloration of *P. s. spilotus* is jet to olive black, with yellow or cream spots in the centre of the majority of scales; in most specimens these spots are arranged in diamond-like clusters along the body. The ventral surface is cream to yellow with dark blotches. In *P. s. variegatus* and *P. s. imbricatus* the dorsal coloration is extremely variable, but most commonly is light to dark brown with irregular, broad bands and blotches which are usually lighter, centred and edged with black. The ventral surface is cream to yellow with dark blotches.

The head is covered with small irregular scales; mid-body scales are in 40 to 51 rows; ventrals number 240 to 310; subcaudals are mostly divided, numbering 60 to 95; anal scale is usually single.

Maximum length is about 4.2 metres.

REMARKS: Most common in the heavily timbered, coastal regions, this nocturnal arboreal species is secretive during the day, excepting for the early morning when it often emerges to bask. As in all pythons it is oviparous (egg-laying) and may lay up to 47 eggs in a clutch; the female coils about the eggs to aid in the incubation and to protect them. Newly hatched young measure about 300 mm and weigh about 15 grams. Constriction is used to overpower their prey, which consists of mammals, birds and occasionally lizards. All forms are unpredictable in temperament, particularly *P. s. variegatus,* which often bites savagely with little provocation. In northern New South Wales where the Diamond and Carpet Pythons are sympatric, hybridisation occurs, resulting in a mixed colour phase or integrade.

SUBSPECIES:

Python spilotus spilotus (Lacépède, 1804)
Restricted to the New South Wales coastal strip.

Python spilotus imbricatus (Smith, 1981)
Found in the south-west of Western Australia. Differs from *P. s. variegatus* in having strongly imbricate, lanceolate dorsal scales, fewer ventrals and fewer subcaudals.

Python spilotus variegatus (Gray, 1824)
Found from the Kimberleys of Western Australia, through the top end of the Northern Territory, most of Queensland and New South Wales to southern parts of South Australia.

FAMILY ACROCHORDIDAE

(Harmless Aquatic Snakes)

GENUS *ACROCHORDUS*

Little File Snake **Plate 8**
Acrochordus granulatus (Schneider, 1799)

RANGE: The north Australian coast from about Derby, Western Australia, to Ingham, Queensland. Also found in south-east Asia.

IDENTIFICATION: Head barely distinct from neck; robust, compressed body; prehensile tail. Body coloration is brownish-black, with numerous narrow pale fawn or whitish cross-bands.

Body scales small and spinose, in 85 to 105 rows at mid-body; no distinct ventral or subcaudal scales; a distinct median ventral fold present.

Maximum length is about 1.2 metres.

REMARKS: An aquatic species which is totally marine, being most common in estuarine waters. Normally nocturnal, it spends most of the day burrowed into soft sand or mud, or squeezed tightly under bottom debris, ascending only occasionally to breathe. It feeds upon small fish, prefering such bottom dwellers as gobies (*Gobiidae*) and mudskippers (*Periophthalmus*). It bears live young and may produce up to 12 in a litter; newborn young measure about 280 mm in length.

Javan File Snake **Plate 9**

Acrochordus javanicus Hornstedt, 1787

RANGE: Far northern Australia, from Derby, Western Australia, to Cairns, Queensland. Also found in south-east Asia.

IDENTIFICATION: Head barely distinct from neck; robust, compressed body; prehensile tail. Dorsal coloration is brownish with darker variegated markings. Ventral surface is whitish.

Loose, flaccid skin comprised of small spinose scales; mid-body scales in 120 to 155 rows; no distinct ventral or subcaudal scales.

Maximum length is about 2.5 metres.

REMARKS: This peculiar aquatic snake is virtually helpless if stranded out of the water. Whilst most common in freshwater rivers and billabongs, it is not unusual to encounter it in the sea or in estuaries. Sometimes found in colonies, it prefers dark overhanging banks where it can anchor its tail firmly around pandanus roots, then with fore-body extended and swaying with the current, it strikes at passing fish. It is normally nocturnal and bears live young, producing up to 40 in a litter. Non-venomous and completely harmless, it is often hunted by Aborigines who utilise it as a food item.

FAMILY COLUBRIDAE
SUBFAMILY BOIGINAE

(Rear-fanged Tree Snake)

GENUS *BOIGA*

Brown Tree Snake **Plate 9**
Boiga irregularis (Merrem, 1802)

RANGE: Coastal northern and eastern Australia. Also found in New Guinea and Indonesia.

IDENTIFICATION: Broad head distinct from the neck; slender body. Dorsal coloration is variable and may be cream, brown or reddish-brown with numerous red, brown or blackish cross-bands on the body and tail. Ventral surface is cream to salmon.

Mid-body scales are in 19 to 23 rows; ventrals number 225 to 265; subcaudals are divided, numbering 85 to 130; anal scale is single.

Maximum length is about two metres.

REMARKS: A nocturnal arboreal species which may congregate in small colonies residing in rock ledges and hollow tree limbs. It is an egg-layer and may produce up to 12 eggs in a clutch; newly hatched young measure about 280 mm in length. It feeds upon lizards, small mammals, birds and occasionally bird eggs; if it has trouble subduing large prey it may resort to constriction. When provoked it becomes very aggressive, raising the forebody in a series of loops and with open mouth will strike repeatedly. Although venomous, it is not regarded as dangerous to humans.

SUBFAMILY COLUBRINAE

(Harmless Land Snakes)

GENUS *AMPHIESMA*

Freshwater Snake or Keelback **Plate 10**
Amphiesma mairii (Grey, 1841)

RANGE: Coastal northern Australia, from the Kimberleys in Western Australia to northern New South Wales.

IDENTIFICATION: Head distinct from neck; moderately robust body. Dorsal coloration is variable and may be grey, olive, brown, black or reddish, liberally peppered with dark markings. Ventral surface may be cream, olive, brown or salmon with or without black-edged scales.

Mid-body scales keeled in 15 or 17 rows; ventrals number 130 to 165; subcaudals are divided, numbering 50 to 85; anal scale is divided.

Maximum length is about one metre.

REMARKS: Although always found within close proximity to permanent water, this species is not totally aquatic. Active by day or night, it feeds principally upon frogs and tadpoles but occasionally takes small lizards and fish. It is an egg-layer and may produce up to 17 eggs in a clutch; newly hatched young measure about 140 mm in length. If grasped by the tail, this species has the ability to dismember the tail and make good its escape, a defence mechanism usually employed by lizards. When agitated it inflates itself displaying blue skin between the scales. Although it bites as a last resort it is non-venomous and completely harmless.

GENUS *DENDRELAPHIS*

Northern Tree Snake
Dendrelaphis calligaster (Günther, 1867)

RANGE: Eastern Cape York Peninsula, Queensland. Also found in Torres Strait Islands and New Guinea.

IDENTIFICATION: Head slightly distinct from neck; slender, elongate body. Dorsal coloration is olive to brown, with a distinct dark streak on the side of the head. Ventral surface is yellow peppered with black.

Mid-body scales are in 13 or 15 rows; ventrals number 180 to 230; subcaudals are divided, numbering 90 to 150; anal scale is divided.

Maximum length is about 1.2 metres.

REMARKS: An agile arboreal species which inhabits the rainforest region of Cape York Peninsula. It is an egg-layer but nothing is known of clutch sizes; it feeds upon frogs and small lizards. Being non-venomous, it relies upon speed in swallowing to overpower its prey, which are often seen still struggling when halfway down the snake's body. Completely harmless.

Common Tree Snake **Plates 10, 11**

Dendrelaphis punctulatus (Gray, 1827)

RANGE: Coastal regions of northern and eastern Australia.

IDENTIFICATION: Head slightly distinct from the neck; slender body. Dorsal coloration varies geographically. The most common form in New South Wales and Queensland is green dorsally and yellow ventrally; other north Queensland forms are dark brown to black dorsally, yellow ventrally, to an entirely blue-coloured form. Northern Territory and Western Australian specimens are golden yellow with a bluish head.

Mid-body scales are in 13 or 15 rows; ventrals number 180 to 230; subcaudals are divided, numbering 90 to 150; anal scale is divided.

Maximum length is about two metres.

REMARKS: An arboreal diurnal species which prefers heavily timbered areas. It may be found in hollow limbs, rock crevices or beneath debris, sometimes in small colonies. It is an egg-layer and may produce up to 14 eggs in a clutch; newly hatched young measure about 330 mm in length. A voracious feeder, it preys upon frogs, tadpoles, small lizards and occasionally fish; one specimen showed ophiophagous (snake-eating) tendencies by consuming a Broad-headed Snake *Hoplocephalus bungaroides*. This agile species, which is also a competent swimmer, has a distinctive defensive posture which involves raising the forebody and inflating the neck and body, displaying blue skin between the scales. If further provoked it releases a strong-smelling odour from its anal glands, this species is non-venomous and completely harmless.

GENUS *STEGONOTUS*

Slaty-grey Snake **Plate 11**
Stegonotus cucullatus (Duméril, Bibron & Duméril, 1854)

RANGE: Far northern Queensland and the "Top End" of the Northern Territory.

IDENTIFICATION: Head distinct from the neck; moderately slender body. Dorsal coloration is polished slate-grey to black; ventral surface white or creamish.

Mid-body scales are in 17 or 19 rows; ventrals number 170 to 225; subcaudals are divided, numbering 60 to 105; anal scale is single.

Maximum length is about two metres.

REMARKS: A nocturnal species which is usually found in close proximity to permanent water. It is a competent swimmer and climber and feeds upon frogs, lizards and small mammals. An egg-layer, it may produce up to 16 eggs in a clutch; newly hatched young measure about 330 mm in length. Aggressive, if provoked, it will bite savagely at every opportunity, and often releases a foul-smelling odour from its anal glands. It is non-venomous and completely harmless.

SUBFAMILY HOMALOPSINAE

(Rear-fanged Aquatic Snakes)

GENUS *CERBERUS*

Bockadam **Plate 12**
Cerberus australis (Gray, 1849)

RANGE: Coastal northern Australia, from western Cape

York Peninsula, Queensland, to Derby, Western Australia.

IDENTIFICATION: Broad head distinct from the neck; valvular nostrils on top of the snout; moderately stout body. Dorsal coloration is grey or reddish with numerous irregular dark cross-bars and streaks. Two dark streaks are present on the head, one through the eye and another from the corner of the mouth to the side of the neck. Ventral surface is cream, yellow or salmon with irregular dark bands and blotches.

Mid-body scales are in 23 or 25 rows; ventrals number 140 to 160; subcaudals are divided, numbering 45 to 60; anal scale is divided.

Maximum length is about 1.2 metres.

REMARKS: A nocturnal aquatic species which is normally found in estuaries and mangrove flats, sometimes in small colonies. At low tide it burrows into soft mud, leaving just the top of the head and prominent eyes visible. It preys principally upon mudskippers (family: Periophthalmidae), but also feeds upon other small fish and crustaceans. A live-bearer, it may have up to 26 young in a litter; newborn young measure about 180 mm in length. Bockadams have an unpredictable temperament, often biting unexpectedly. The author was the recipient of a bite from a large specimen, which resulted in local stinging. Although venomous, this rear-fanged species is regarded as harmless to humans.

Plate 12

Cerberus rhynchops novaeguineae (Loveridge, 1948)

RANGE: Normally found in New Guinea, at least one specimen of this subspecies has been collected in Australia, from Edward River on the western side of Cape York Peninsula.

IDENTIFICATION: Broad head distinct from the neck; valvular nostrils on top of the snout; moderately stout body. Dorsal coloration is light grey with numerous irregular dark cross-bars and streaks. The head has a few scattered dark spots. Ventral surface is creamish with irregular dark bands and blotches.

Mid-body scales are in 23 or 25 rows; ventrals number 145 to 150; subcaudals are mostly divided, numbering 43 to 49; anal scale is divided.

Maximum length is about 850 mm.

REMARKS: A nocturnal aquatic species which inhabits mangrove flats along estuaries, creeks and rivers. It preys upon small fish, particularly mudskippers (family: Periophthalmidae), which it hunts on mud flats exposed at low tide. It is a live-bearer, but the exact number of young is unknown. Although venomous, and rear-fanged, it is regarded as harmless to humans.

GENUS *ENHYDRIS*

Macleay's Water Snake — Plate 13

Enhydris macleayi (Ogilby, 1891)

RANGE: North-eastern Queensland.

IDENTIFICATION: Head distinct from the neck; moderately stout body. Dorsal coloration is polished grey or brown, with a light stripe from the rostral, along the side of the head and neck. The posterior two-thirds of the body have numerous wavy black cross-bars. A black streak extends along the lower sides of the body. A broad black stripe is present on the undersurface of the tail.

Mid-body scales are in 21 or 23 rows; ventrals number 147 to 152; subcaudals are divided, numbering 36 to 46; anal scale is divided.

Maximum length is about one metre.

REMARKS: A nocturnal aquatic species which is found only in fresh water, such as billabongs, creeks and rivers. In still water it often shelters among the matted roots of floating plants. It is a live-bearer and should produce similar litters to *Enhydris polylepis*. It feeds upon fish, frogs and tadpoles. Although venomous, this rear-fanged species is regarded as harmless to humans.

GENUS *FORDONIA*

White-bellied Mangrove Snake **Plate 13**
Fordonia leucobalia (Schlegel, 1837)

RANGE: Coastal northern Australia, also found in New Guinea, south-east Asia, the Philippines and Cochin China.

IDENTIFICATION: Broad head distinct from the neck; robust body. Dorsal coloration is extremely variable, with six colour phases being recorded. The three most common phases are uniformly black, black with variegated white blotches or reddish with white or bluish variegated blotches. Ventral surface is white or creamish, with a black stripe on the undersurface of the tail.

Mid-body scales are in 23 to 29 rows; ventrals number 130 to 160; subcaudals are mostly divided, numbering 25 to 45; anal scale is divided.

Maximum length is about one metre.

REMARKS: A nocturnal aquatic species which inhabits mangrove flats along estuaries, creeks and rivers. At low tide it shelters among mangrove roots or down crab holes. It feeds upon small crustaceans and when hunting forages amongst dense mangrove roots, broken pools and channels. The author has recorded it feeding on fiddler crabs (genus: *Uca*) and the shrimp *Thalassina anomala*. It is a live-bearer and produces about 8 young in a litter; newborn young measure about 180 mm in length. Completely inoffensive by nature, even when provoked, and, although a venomous rear-fanged snake, it is regarded as harmless to humans.

GENUS *MYRON*

Richardson's Mangrove Snake

Myron richardsonii Gray, 1849

RANGE: Coastal northern Australia, from the Gulf of Carpentaria to about Derby, Western Australia. Also found in New Guinea.

IDENTIFICATION: Head slightly distinct from the neck; moderately robust body. Dorsal coloration is light to dark olive-grey with numerous irregular dark cross-bands on the body and tail. Ventral surface is cream or yellow, mottled with black or brown.

Mid-body scales are in 21 or 23 rows; ventrals number 130 to 145; subcaudals are divided, numbering 30 to 40; anal scale is divided.

Maximum length is about 500 mm.

REMARKS: A nocturnal aquatic species which inhabits the mangrove-fringed mud flats of tidal estuaries, creeks and rivers. It shelters down crab holes or among mangrove roots, often in small colonies. When hunting, it forages in and around broken water pools, feeding upon small fish and crustaceans. It is a live-bearer and may produce about 8 young in a litter; newborn young measure about 120 mm in length. Although a rear-fanged venomous species, it is regarded as harmless to humans.

FAMILY ELAPIDAE

(Front-fanged Land Snakes)

GENUS *ACANTHOPHIS*

Common Death Adder **Plate 14**
Acanthophis antarcticus (Shaw, 1794)

(See Dangerous Species section p. 83.)

Northern Death Adder
Acanthophis praelongus Ramsay, 1877

(See Dangerous Species section p. 84.)

Desert Death Adder **Plate 15**
Acanthophis pyrrhus Boulenger, 1898

(See Dangerous Species section p. 85.)

GENUS *AUSTRELAPS*

Copperhead **Plates 15, 16**
Austrelaps superbus (Günther, 1858)

(See Dangerous Species section p. 86.)

GENUS *BRACHYASPIS*

Bardick
Brachyaspis curta (Schlegel, 1837)

(See Dangerous Species section p. 87.)

White-crowned Snake **Plate 16**
Cacophis harrietae Krefft, 1896

RANGE: Coastal south-eastern Queensland to coastal north-eastern New South Wales.

IDENTIFICATION: Head distinct from the neck; moderately slender body. Dorsal coloration is greyish to dark brown, with a white or creamish stripe around the head which is widest on the nape, forming a distinct collar. Ventral surface is dark grey.

Mid-body scales are in 15 rows; ventrals number 170 to 200; subcaudals are divided, numbering 25 to 45; anal scale is divided.

Maximum length is about 490 mm.

REMARKS: A colourful nocturnal snake which is often discovered moving about on warm nights. It is oviparous and may produce up to 10 eggs in a clutch; the young when hatched measure about 140 mm. The largest male on record is 346 mm, which is approximately 30 per cent smaller than the largest female. It feeds mainly upon small lizards, but has also been recorded eating lizard eggs and blind snakes (family: Typhlopidae). When alarmed or provoked it may assume a defensive posture, in which it raises the forebody off the ground but points the head downwards, thus displaying its colourful head markings. It is venomous, but not regarded as dangerous to humans.

Dwarf Crowned Snake **Plate 17**
Cacophis krefftii Günther, 1863

RANGE: Northern coastal regions of New South Wales, from about Gosford to the south-eastern corner of Queensland.

IDENTIFICATION: Head slightly distinct from neck; moderately slender body. Dorsal coloration is black to brownish-black, with a white or yellowish stripe around the head, which is most prominent on the nape. Ventral surface is creamish patterned with black, a black line divides the subcaudals.

Mid-body scales are in 15 rows; ventrals number 140 to 160; subcaudals are divided, numbering 25 to 40; anal scale is divided.

Maximum length is about 330 mm.

REMARKS: This small nocturnal snake is often found in or under rotting logs, it is oviparous and may produce up to 5 eggs in a clutch; the young when hatched measure about 100 mm. This is another species in which females exceed males in length; the largest male recorded was 287 mm. It appears to feed entirely upon small scincid lizards. When alarmed it assumes a defensive posture similar to that of *Cacophis harrietae*. It is venomous but is too small to be regarded as harmful to humans.

Golden-crowned Snake **Plate 17**

Cacophis squamulosus (Duméril, Bibron & Duméril, 1854)

RANGE: Coastally from central Queensland, to the Wollongong district in New South Wales. In the Sydney area it is most common in the northern suburbs.

IDENTIFICATION: Head distinct from neck; moderately slender body. Dorsal coloration is dark brown to blackish, with a yellowish stripe around the head which extends well back on the nape, but fails to meet to form a collar. Ventral surface is pink to reddish patterned with black, a black line divides the subcaudals.

Mid-body scales are in 15 rows; ventrals number 165 to 185; subcaudals are divided, numbering 30 to 50; anal scale is divided.

Maximum length is about 715 mm.

REMARKS: This beautiful nocturnal species is often found beneath large well-embedded rocks. It is oviparous and may produce up to 14 eggs in a clutch; the young when hatched measure about 160 mm. The largest male recorded was 482 mm, which is approximately 32 per cent smaller than the largest female. It feeds mainly upon small lizards, but has also been recorded feeding upon lizard eggs, blind snakes (family: Typhlopidae) and small frogs. When alarmed it assumes the typical defence posture of the genus (see *Cacophis harrietae*); it is venomous but not normally regarded as harmful to humans.

GENUS *CRYPTOPHIS*

Small-eyed Snake **Plate 18**

Cryptophis nigrescens (Günther, 1858)

(See Dangerous Species section p. 88.)

Secretive Snake **Plate 18**

Cryptophis pallidiceps (Günther, 1858)

RANGE: The "Top End" of the Northern Territory.

IDENTIFICATION: Head slightly distinct from neck; moderately slender body. Dorsal coloration is blackish, often with a paler head. The ventral surface can be creamish to pink.

Mid-body scales are in 15 rows; ventrals number 160 to 180; subcaudals are single, numbering 45 to 60; anal scale is single.

Maximum length attained is about 630 mm.

REMARKS: A nocturnal species which shelters beneath rocks, logs and other debris. Nothing has been recorded about its means of reproduction, but being closely related to *Cryptophis nigrescens* it is probably a live-bearer. It feeds mainly upon small lizards but will occasionally take frogs. It is venomous, but not considered dangerous to humans.

GENUS *DEMANSIA*

Black Whip Snake **Plate 19**
Demansia atra (Macleay, 1885)

(See Dangerous Species section p. 88.)

Black Whip Snake (2)
Demansia papuensis melaena Storr, 1978

(See Dangerous Species section p. 89.)

Marble-headed Whip Snake **Plate 19**
Demansia olivacea (Gray, 1842)

RANGE: Mid- and northern coastal areas of Western Australia and the "Top End" of the Northern Territory.

IDENTIFICATION: Head barely distinct from the neck; elongate body. Dorsal coloration is olive-grey, brownish or reddish, often with a dark spot at the base of each scale. The snout and labials are mottled with blackish-brown; a pale-edged dark comma-like marking extends from around the eye to the corner of the mouth. There are usually two grey streaks on the chin, and the throat is spotted with blackish-brown. The remainder of the ventral surface is white or creamish.

Mid-body scales are in 15 rows; ventrals number 160 to 210; subcaudals are divided,

numbering 65 to 105; anal scale is divided.
Maximum length is about 850 mm.

REMARKS: A slender, fast-moving diurnal species which may become semi-nocturnal on warm nights. It occurs in a variety of habitats and preys mostly upon small lizards. It is an egg-layer and Worrell records it producing 3 to 4 in a clutch. Although venomous, it is not regarded as dangerous to humans.

SUBSPECIES: *Demansia olivacea olivacea* (Gray, 1842)
Dorsum brownish, found through the Kimberleys of Western Australia and the "Top End" of the Northern Territory.

Demansia olivacea calodera Storr, 1978
Dorsum olive-grey, a pale-edged dark bar on the nape, found from about Shark Bay to North West Cape on the mid-coast of Western Australia.

Demansia olivacea rufescens Storr, 1978
Dorsum reddish, found in the Pilbara region of Western Australia.

Yellow-faced Whip Snake — Plate 20

Demansia psammophis (Schlegel, 1837)

RANGE: Eastern Australia.

IDENTIFICATION: Head barely distinct from neck; elongate body. Dorsal coloration is greyish to olive-brown, with a pale-edged, dark stripe on the rostral and a similarly coloured comma-like marking surrounding the eye. Ventral surface is creamish to greyish-green.

Mid-body scales are in 15 rows; ventrals number 165 to 230; subcaudals are divided, numbering 60 to 105; anal scale is divided.

Maximum length attained is about one metre.

REMARKS: An extremely active diurnal species which prefers rocky or sandy habitats. It is often found under slabs of rock and occasionally several specimens may be found congregated under the one piece of cover. The main prey item is small lizards, but it also feeds upon other small reptiles and frogs. It is an egg-layer and about 6 eggs are an average clutch. Although venomous, it is not regarded as dangerous to humans.

Plate 20

Demansia reticulata (Gray, 1842)

RANGE: Western Australia (except for far south and far north), southern Northern Territory and northern South Australia.

IDENTIFICATION: Head barely distinct from the neck; elongate body. Dorsal coloration is greenish-grey merging to coppery brown posteriorly; each body scale has prominent black edging giving a distinctive reticulated appearance. The head is olive-green or coppery brown, with a pale-edged dark line running from the rostral to the eyes, where it meets a pale-edged, narrow comma-like marking surrounding the eye. The throat is yellow, while the remainder of the ventral surface is yellowish-white.

Mid-body scales are in 15 rows; ventrals number 172 to 201; subcaudals are divided, numbering 67 to 88; anal scale is divided.

Maximum length attained is about 900 mm.

REMARKS: A fast-moving diurnal species which feeds upon small reptiles and frogs. It is an egg-layer, but there are no records of clutch sizes. Although venomous, it is not regarded as dangerous to humans.

SUBSPECIES: *Demansia reticulata reticulata* (Gray, 1842) Head olive-green, found in the south-west coastal area of Western Australia.

Demansia reticulata cupreiceps Storr, 1978 Head coppery brown, found in Western Australia (except for far south and far north), southern Northern Territory and northern South Australia.

Collared Whip Snake **Plate 21**

Demansia torquata (Günther, 1862)

RANGE: North-eastern Australia, from around the New South Wales/Queensland border to the Western Australia/Northern Territory border.

IDENTIFICATION: Head barely distinct from the neck; elongate body. Dorsal coloration can be olive-brown to greyish; the head markings are variable but normally the top of the head is dark with one or more yellow- or orange-edged dark bands across the neck. A pale-edged dark stripe rounds the rostral and a similarly coloured comma-like marking surrounds the eye. The ventral surface is greyish and there may be some darker mottling under the chin.

Mid-body scales are in 15 rows; ventrals number 185 to 220; subcaudals are divided, numbering 70 to 90; anal scale is divided.

Maximum length is about 850 mm.

REMARKS: A fast-moving diurnal species which can be found in a variety of habitats. It feeds mainly upon small lizards but will also take other small reptiles. It is an egg-layer but little has been recorded about clutch sizes. Although venomous, it is not regarded as dangerous to humans.

De Vis' Banded Snake **Plate 21**
Denisonia devisii Waite & Longman, 1920

RANGE: From south-western and central New South Wales to central northern Queensland.

IDENTIFICATION: Broad, depressed head, distinct from neck; robust body. Dorsal coloration is light brown with dark irregular cross-bands on the body and tail; the head is dark brown with distinctly striped labials. Ventral surface is creamish.

Mid-body scales are in 17 rows; ventrals number 120 to 150; subcaudals are single, numbering 20 to 40; anal scale is single.

Maximum length is about 500 mm.

REMARKS: A nocturnal species which may be found beneath logs, rubbish and other debris or down deep earth cracks. It is a live-bearer and may have up to 8 young in a litter; it feeds mainly upon small lizards but has been recorded taking frogs and newborn mice. If provoked it becomes very agitated and aggressive, flattening the body and biting at every opportunity. It is venomous and although not considered dangerous, a bite can be most painful.

Rosen's Snake
Denisonia fasciata Rosén, 1905

RANGE: Most of southern Western Australia.

IDENTIFICATION: Head depressed, distinct from the neck; robust body. Dorsal coloration is light brown with dark irregular cross-bands on the body and tail; there is a dark streak from the rostral, through the eye to the neck. The labials are uniformly whitish. Ventral surface is white or cream.

Mid-body scales are in 17 rows; ventrals number 144 to 182; subcaudals are single, numbering 20 to 38; anal scale is single.

Maximum length is about 615 mm.

REMARKS: A nocturnal terrestrial species which may be found in a variety of habitats. Virtually nothing is known of its reproductive habits and the only recorded prey items are small lizards. It is venomous, but not regarded as dangerous to humans.

Ornamental Snake **Plate 22**
Denisonia maculata (Steindachner, 1867)

(See Dangerous Species section p. 90.)

Little Spotted Snake **Plate 22**
Denisonia punctata Boulenger, 1896

RANGE: Northern Australia, with the exception of eastern Queensland.

IDENTIFICATION: Head depressed, slightly distinct from the neck; moderately slender body. Dorsal coloration is light to reddish brown, often with a darker spot on each scale. The head and neck have prominent dark blotches. Ventral surface is white or creamish.

Mid-body scales are in 15 rows; ventrals number 146 to 183; subcaudals are single, numbering 23 to 42; anal scale is single.

Maximum length is about 520 mm.

REMARKS: A nocturnal species which is usually associated with red desert areas. It is a live-bearer with one litter of 5 being recorded; it preys mainly upon small lizards, but has also been recorded feeding on blind snakes (family: Typhlopidae). It is venomous and while not considered dangerous, its bite can be most painful.

GENUS *DRYSDALIA*

Crowned Snake or Werr **Plate 23**
Drysdalia coronata (Schlegel, 1837)

RANGE: South-western Western Australia.

IDENTIFICATION: Head slightly distinct from the neck; moderately slender body. Dorsal coloration is pale, olive or dark brown to greyish; the head is usually dark and has a black stripe forming a crown: this is most prominent on the nape where it forms a distinct collar. The labials are white or creamish. Ventral surface is yellowish.

Mid-body scales are in 15 rows; ventrals number 130 to 160; subcaudals are single, numbering 35 to 55; anal scale is single.

Maximum length is about 550 mm.

REMARKS: This species is mainly nocturnal, being most active on warm evenings. It is a live-bearer and may have up to 9 in a litter; newborn young normally measure about 130 mm. It feeds upon frogs, small lizards and occasionally insects. Although venomous, it is not regarded as dangerous to humans.

White-lipped Snake **Plate 23**
Drysdalia coronoides (Günther, 1858)

RANGE: South-eastern Australia and Tasmania; in New South Wales it extends along the higher parts of the northern tablelands.

IDENTIFICATION: Head slightly distinct from the neck; moderately slender body. Dorsal coloration is variable being any shade of grey, olive-green, brown or reddish. Two streaks, one black and the other white, run along the side of the head to the neck. Ventral surface may be creamish, yellowish or pinkish.

Mid-body scales are in 15 rows; ventrals number 130 to 160; subcaudals are single, numbering 35 to 60; anal scale is single.

Maximum length is about 500 mm.

REMARKS: Although mainly nocturnal, this species may occasionally be encountered foraging during the day. It is a live-bearer and may have up to 10 young in a litter; the newborn young normally measure about 100 mm. It feeds mainly upon small lizards, but has also been recorded eating skink eggs and frogs. Although venomous, it is not regarded as dangerous to humans.

Plate 24

Drysdalia rhodogaster (Jan, 1863)

RANGE: South-eastern New South Wales

IDENTIFICATION: Head distinct from the neck; robust body. Dorsal coloration is olive to brownish; the head is black on top with a mottled snout; there is a narrow black stripe from the nostril to the eye and another, more indistinct, black stripe from below the eye to the neck. A prominent orange or light brown band is present on the nape. Ventral surface can be yellow to orange.

Mid-body scales are in 15 rows; ventrals number 141 to 155; subcaudals are single, numbering 41 to 54; anal scale is single.

Maximum size is about 460 mm.

REMARKS: This species is normally diurnal, but does

become semi-nocturnal during warm weather. It prefers dry habitats and may be found sheltering under rocks, logs and other debris. It is a live-bearer and may produce up to 6 young which are about 110 mm long at birth. It feeds almost entirely on small skinks and although venomous, is regarded as harmless to humans.

GENUS *ELAPOGNATHUS*

Little Brown Snake
Elapognathus minor (Günther, 1863)

RANGE: Only found in a limited area of the south-west corner of Western Australia.

IDENTIFICATION: Head slightly distinct from the neck; robust body. Dorsal coloration is olive-brown with blackish skin between the scales. The supralabials are yellowish and there is often a yellowish to blackish collar on the nape. Ventral surface is creamy yellow to greenish with a black area on each scale.

Mid-body scales are in 15 rows; ventrals number 120 to 130; subcaudals are single, numbering 50 to 70; anal scale is single.

Maximum length is about 450 mm.

REMARKS: Very little is known about this rare species; it is venomous but regarded as harmless to humans.

GENUS *FURINA*

Red-naped Snake **Plate 24**
Furina diadema (Schlegel, 1837)

RANGE: Coastal and inland New South Wales to southern Queensland.

IDENTIFICATION: Head slightly distinct from the neck; slender body. Dorsal coloration is reddish-brown, with each scale being dark-edged giving a reticulated appearance. The head and neck are shiny black with a red crescent-shaped mark on the nape. Ventral surface is white or cream.

Mid-body scales are in 15 rows; ventrals number 160 to 210; subcaudals are divided, numbering 35 to 70; anal scale is divided.

Maximum length is about 450 mm.

REMARKS: A common nocturnal snake which is usually found under rocks, logs and other ground debris. In favourable habitats it is not uncommon to find several specimens occupying the same site. This is an oviparous species which may lay up to 10 eggs in a clutch. It feeds upon small lizards and occasionally insects and although venomous, it is considered harmless to humans.

GENUS *GLYPHODON*

Dunmall's Snake **Plate 25**

Glyphodon dunmalli Worrell, 1955

RANGE: Inland south-eastern Queensland

IDENTIFICATION: Head distinct from the neck; moderately robust body. Dorsal coloration is uniform dark slaty brown. Ventral surface is white.

Mid-body scales are in 21 rows; ventrals number 175 to 190; subcaudals are divided, numbering 35 to 50; anal scale is divided.

Maximum length is about 750 mm.

REMARKS: This is a rare species about which little is known. It is nocturnal and feeds mainly upon small lizards. Inoffensive in temperament, it is disinclined to bite unless provoked. Although venomous and not regarded as dangerous to man, a bite sustained by the author resulted in intense stinging around the bitten area, followed by swelling of the entire hand.

Brown-headed Snake **Plate 25**
Glyphodon tristis Günther, 1858

RANGE: Eastern Cape York Peninsula; also found in Torres Strait islands and New Guinea.

IDENTIFICATION: Head indistinct from the neck; moderately robust body. Dorsal coloration is dark brown to black with distinct white edging on each scale; a brownish-yellow collar crosses the nape. Ventral surface is white or creamish, with some dark markings on the chin and subcaudals.

Mid-body scales are in 17 rows; ventrals number 160 to 190; subcaudals are divided, numbering 30 to 60; anal scale is divided.

Maximum length is about 900 mm.

REMARKS: A little-known nocturnal species which shelters under logs and other ground debris. It feeds upon small lizards and is nervous and aggressive if molested. Although venomous, it is not regarded as dangerous to humans.

GENUS *HEMIASPIS*

Grey Snake **Plate 26**
Hemiaspis damelii (Günther, 1876)

RANGE: Inland New South Wales, through inland south-eastern Queensland to the coast at about Rockhampton.

IDENTIFICATION: Head slightly distinct from the neck; moderately robust body. Dorsal coloration is grey to olive-grey, often with a black spot at the base of each scale. The head is black, although in mature specimens this often fades to a dark collar on the nape. Ventral surface is creamish with occasional grey spots.

Mid-body scales are in 17 rows; ventrals number 140 to 170; subcaudals are single, numbering 35 to 50; anal scale is divided.

Maximum length is about 750 mm.

REMARKS: Normally diurnal, this species may become semi-nocturnal during warm weather. It is a live-bearer and may produce up to 12 young, which are about 160 mm long at birth. It feeds upon small lizards and frogs. It is inoffensive in temperament and although venomous, is not regarded as dangerous to humans.

Marsh Snake — Plates 26, 27

Hemiaspis signata (Jan, 1859)

RANGE: Coastal eastern Australia.

IDENTIFICATION: Head slightly distinct from the neck; moderately robust body. Dorsal coloration is brown to olive, often with a darker head. There are two distinct white or yellowish streaks on each side of the head, one on the supralabials and the other from the eye to the neck. Ventral surface is black or dark grey. A black melanotic form is fairly common in New South Wales.

Mid-body scales are in 17 rows; ventrals number 150 to 170; subcaudals are single, numbering 40 to 60; anal scale is divided.

Maximum length is about 900 mm.

REMARKS: This common species prefers swampy habitats and in favourable areas may congregate in small colonies. Although mainly diurnal, it does become semi-nocturnal during warm weather. It is a live-bearer and may produce up to 20 young, which measure about 110 mm at birth. Normally feeding upon small lizards and frogs, it has also been recorded eating other smaller snakes. It is venomous and although not considered dangerous, large specimens can deliver a painful bite.

GENUS *HOPLOCEPHALUS*

Pale-headed Snake **Plate 27**
Hoplocephalus bitorquatus (Jan, 1859)

(See Dangerous Species section p. 91.)

Broad-headed Snake **Plate 28**
Hoplocephalus bungaroides (Boie, 1828)

(See Dangerous Species section p. 92.)

Stephen's Banded Snake **Plates 28, 29**
Hoplocephalus stephensi Krefft, 1869

(See Dangerous Species section p. 93.)

GENUS *NEELAPS*

Long-nosed Snake
Neelaps bimaculatus (Duméril, Bibron & Duméril, 1854)

RANGE: Southern Western Australia and south-western South Australia.

IDENTIFICATION: Head indistinct from the neck; moderately robust body. Dorsal coloration is pinkish to pale orange or reddish-brown, with each scale having dark edging. Two dark blotches on the head and nape are separated by two to five scales. Ventral surface is creamish.

Mid-body scales are in 15 rows; ventrals number 175 to 235; subcaudals are divided, numbering 15 to 35; anal scale is divided.

Maximum length is about 450 mm.

REMARKS: Virtually unknown, it is a burrowing species, which, although venomous, is too small to be harmful to humans.

Beaded Snake
Neelaps calonotus (Duméril, Bibron & Duméril, 1854)

RANGE: Only known from a narrow coastal strip near Perth, Western Australia.

IDENTIFICATION: Head indistinct from the neck; moderately robust body. Dorsal coloration is creamish, with each scale having pink or reddish-orange edges. The snout is tipped with black; two dark blotches on the head and nape are separated by two or three scales. A vertebral stripe, composed of dark scales with white centres, extends from the nape to the tail tip. Ventral surface is creamish.

Mid-body scales are in 15 rows; ventrals number 120 to 150; subcaudals are divided, numbering 20 to 40; anal scale is divided.

Maximum length is about 285 mm.

REMARKS: Virtually unknown, it is a burrowing species which, although venomous, is regarded as harmless to humans.

GENUS *NOTECHIS*

Black Tiger Snake **Plates 29, 30**
Notechis ater (Krefft, 1866)

(See Dangerous Species section p. 94.)

Common Tiger Snake **Plate 31**
Notechis scutatus (Peters, 1861)

(See Dangerous Species section p. 95.)

GENUS *OXYURANUS*

Small-scaled Snake or Western Taipan **Plate 32**
Oxyuranus microlepidota (McCoy, 1879)

(See Dangerous Species section p. 96.)

Taipan **Plate 32**
Oxyuranus scutellatus (Peters, 1867)

(See Dangerous Species section p. 97.)

GENUS *PSEUDECHIS*

Mulga or King Brown Snake **Plate 33**
Pseudechis australis (Gray, 1842)

(See Dangerous Species section p. 99.)

Collett's Snake
Pseudechis colletti Boulenger, 1902

(See Dangerous Species section p. 100.)

Blue-bellied or Spotted Black Snake **Plate 33**
Pseudechis guttatus De Vis, 1905

(See Dangerous Species section p. 100.)

Red-bellied Black Snake **Plate 34**
Pseudechis porphyriacus (Shaw, 1794)

(See Dangerous Species section p. 101.)

GENUS *PSEUDONAJA*

Dugite **Plate 34**
Pseudonaja affinis Günther, 1872

(See Dangerous Species section p. 102.)

Speckled Brown Snake **Plate 35**
Pseudonaja guttata (Parker, 1926)

(See Dangerous Species section p. 103.)

Ingram's Brown Snake **Plate 35**
Pseudonaja ingrami (Boulenger, 1908)

(See Dangerous Species section p. 104.)

Ringed Brown Snake **Plate 36**
Pseudonaja modesta Günther, 1872

(See Dangerous Species section p. 105.)

Western Brown Snake **Plate 36**
Pseudonaja nuchalis Günther, 1858

(See Dangerous Species section p. 106.)

Common Brown Snake **Plate 37**
Pseudonaja textilis (Duméril, Bibron & Duméril, 1854)

(See Dangerous Species section p. 107.)

GENUS *RHINOPLOCEPHALUS*

Muller's Snake

Rhinoplocephalus bicolor Muller, 1885

RANGE: Found only in the south-west corner of Western Australia.

IDENTIFICATION: Head barely distinct from the neck; moderately robust body. Dorsal coloration is dark grey merging to yellowish-orange on the sides, the head is usually darker than the body. Ventral surface is white or creamish.

Mid-body scales are in 15 rows; ventrals number 145 to 165; subcaudals are single, numbering 25 to 35; anal scale is single.

Maximum length is about 400 mm.

REMARKS: Very little is known about this rare species. It is a secretive, burrowing species that has been recorded feeding upon frogs but it is most probable that small lizards are its principal prey item. Although venomous, it is not regarded as dangerous to humans.

GENUS *SIMOSELAPS*

Northern Desert Banded Snake

Simoselaps anomala (Sternfeld, 1919)

RANGE: Central Australia and northern parts of Western Australia.

IDENTIFICATION: Head indistinct from the neck; robust body. Dorsal coloration is yellow to reddish with numerous dark cross-bands on the body and tail. The head is mottled and has an indistinct light bar separating a dark head blotch from a dark bar on the nape. Ventral surface is creamish.

Mid-body scales are in 15 rows; ventrals number 119 to 130; subcaudals are divided, numbering 17 to 27; anal scale is divided.

Maximum length is about 210 mm.

REMARKS: Virtually unknown, it should be similar to *Simoselaps bertholdi*.

Simoselaps approximans (Glauert, 1954)

RANGE: North-western Western Australia.

IDENTIFICATION: Head indistinct from the neck; robust body. Dorsal coloration is whitish, with numerous broad dark cross-bands on the body and tail. Ventral surface is creamish.

Mid-body scales are in 17 rows; ventrals number 158 to 181; subcaudals are divided, numbering 19 to 27; anal scale is divided.

Maximum length is about 370 mm.

REMARKS: Virtually unknown, it should be similar to *Simoselaps semifasciatus*.

Australian Coral Snake **Plate 38**
Simoselaps australis (Krefft, 1864)

RANGE: From south-eastern South Australia, through central New South Wales and south-eastern Queensland to coastal areas of northern New South Wales and southern Queensland.

IDENTIFICATION: Head indistinct from the neck; robust body; shovel-shaped snout. Dorsal coloration is any shade of pink to red with numerous cross-bands formed of cream, centred dark-edged scales on the body and tail. There is a broad black bar across the top of the head and another across the nape. Ventral surface is whitish.

Mid-body scales are in 17 rows; ventrals number 140 to 170; subcaudals are divided, numbering 15 to 30; anal scale is divided.

Maximum length is about 500 mm.

REMARKS: This beautifully coloured snake is a small, nocturnal burrowing species. During the day it shelters under well-embedded rocks, stumps and logs. Little is known of its reproductive habits, but it has been known to feed on small lizards. Although venomous, it is regarded as harmless to humans.

Desert Banded Snake **Plate 38**

Simoselaps bertholdi Jan, 1859

RANGE: Southern parts of Western Australia and South Australia.

IDENTIFICATION: Head indistinct from the neck; robust body. Dorsal coloration is yellow to reddish with numerous dark cross-bands on the body and tail. The head is mottled with an indistinct light bar separating a dark head blotch from a dark neck bar. Yellow dorsal scales are normally edged with red. Ventral surface is creamish.

Mid-body scales are in 15 rows; ventrals number 100 to 135; subcaudals are divided, numbering 15 to 30; anal scale is divided.

Maximum length is about 330 mm.

REMARKS: Little is known about the habits of this secretive, burrowing species. Waite (1929) records it as being diurnal—"[it] may often be seen basking in the sunshine when the ground is unbearably hot". It is an efficient burrower and can disappear into soft sand very rapidly; it feeds mainly upon small lizards. This snake is feared by Aborigines but, although technically venomous, it is too small to be harmful to humans.

Narrow-banded Burrowing Snake **Plate 39**
Simoselaps fasciolatus (Günther, 1872)

RANGE: Central Australia to southern Western Australia.

IDENTIFICATION: Head indistinct from the neck; robust body. Dorsal coloration is creamish or reddish with numerous narrow dark cross-bands on the body and tail. There is a dark blotch on top of the head and another on the nape. Ventral surface is creamish.

Mid-body scales in 17 rows; ventrals number 140 to 175; subcaudals are divided, numbering 15 to 30; anal scale is divided.

Maximum length is about 400 mm.

REMARKS: A little-known nocturnal burrowing snake, which seems to prefer sandy habitats. Although technically venomous, it is too small to be regarded as harmful to humans.

SUBSPECIES: *Simoselaps fasciolatus fasciolatus* (Günther, 1872)
Found in southern Western Australia, its nuchal bar is more than six scales wide and its cross-bands are one-half to one scale wide.

Simoselaps fasciolatus fasciata (Stirling & Zietz, 1893)
Found in central Australia, its nuchal bar is less than six scales wide and its cross-bands are one and a quarter to two scales wide.

Simoselaps minima (Worrell, 1960)

RANGE: Known only from the vicinity of Broome, north-western Western Australia.

IDENTIFICATION: Head indistinct from the neck; robust body. There is a black bar across the top of the head and another, which is three to four scales wide, on the neck. The rest of the coloration is whitish.

Mid-body scales are in 15 rows; ventrals number 125 to 127; subcaudals are mostly divided, numbering 19 to 22; anal scale is divided.

Maximum length is about 220 mm.

REMARKS: A small, burrowing species, known only from two specimens. Reproductive and feeding habits are unknown. Technically venomous, but regarded as harmless to humans.

Half-girdled Snake — Plate 39

Simoselaps semifasciatus (Günther, 1863)

RANGE: Western and northern Australia.

IDENTIFICATION: Head indistinct from the neck; robust body. Dorsal coloration is light brown to reddish, with numerous dark cross-bands on the body and tail. There is a distinct broad black bar across the top of the head. Ventral surface is whitish.

Mid-body scales are in 17 rows; ventrals number 145 to 190; subcaudals are divided, numbering 14 to 26; anal scale is divided.

Maximum length is about 300 mm.

REMARKS: This small, nocturnal burrowing snake occurs in a variety of habitats. It is secretive and seldom encountered; when seeking shelter it prefers well-embedded rocks, logs and other ground debris. Little is known of its reproductive or feeding habits, but it presumably feeds mostly upon small lizards. Although venomous, it is regarded as harmless to humans.

SUBSPECIES: *Simoselaps semifasciatus roperi* (Kinghorn, 1931).

Found in the Kimberleys of Western Australia,

Northern Territory to north-eastern Queensland. It usually has six supralabials and a semi-divided nasal scale.

Simoselaps semifasciatus semifasciatus (Günther, 1863)
Found in southern Western Australia and north-western South Australia. It usually has five supralabials and an entire nasal scale.

Plate 40

Simoselaps? warro (De Vis, 1884)

RANGE: North-eastern Queensland.

IDENTIFICATION: Head barely distinct from the neck; robust body. Dorsal coloration is yellowish-orange to orange-brown; each scale has darker edging giving a reticulated appearance. The head is dark brown, peppered with cream and there is a broad black collar on the neck. Ventral surface is creamish.

Mid-body scales are in 15 rows; ventrals number 135 to 165; subcaudals are divided, numbering 15 to 25; anal scale is divided.

Maximum length is about 400 mm.

REMARKS: This is a nocturnal burrowing species which, if molested, will flatten its body and thrash about wildly in a display that is purely bluff. It feeds upon small lizards and although venomous, is regarded as harmless to humans.

GENUS *SUTA*

Curl or Myall Snake
Suta suta (Peters, 1863)

Plate 40

(See Dangerous Species section p. 108.)

GENUS *TROPIDECHIS*

Rough-scaled Snake **Plate 41**
Tropidechis carinatus (Krefft, 1863)

(See Dangerous Species section p. 109.)

GENUS *UNECHIS*

Carpentaria Snake **Plate 41**
Unechis carpentariae (Macleay, 1887)

RANGE: Northern and inland eastern Queensland, from about Normanton and Cape York to Maryborough in the south-east.

IDENTIFICATION: Head barely distinct from the neck; moderately slender body. Dorsal coloration is light to dark brown, becoming much lighter on the sides. Ventral surface is creamish.

Mid-body scales are in 15 rows; ventrals number 145 to 190; subcaudals are single, numbering 20 to 35; anal scale is single.

Maximum length is about 600 mm.

REMARKS: Virtually unknown, it is nocturnal and has been recorded feeding upon small lizards. Venomous, but not regarded as dangerous to humans.

Little Whip Snake **Plate 42**
Unechis flagellum (McCoy, 1878)

RANGE: South-eastern New South Wales, Victoria and south-eastern South Australia.

IDENTIFICATION: Head barely distinct from the neck; moderately slender body. Dorsal coloration is brownish, with each scale being darker at its base. The top of the head is black, broken by a pale bar across the snout. Ventral surface is creamish.

Mid-body scales are in 17 (rarely 15) rows; ventrals number 125 to 150; subcaudals are single, numbering 20 to 40; anal scale is single.

Maximum length is about 400 mm.

REMARKS: A small nocturnal species which has been recorded being unearthed from a depth of several centimetres in light sandy soil. It is viviparous (live-bearing), producing about three young in a litter. It feeds mainly upon small lizards, but has also been recorded taking frogs and insects. Although venomous, it may be regarded as harmless to humans.

Black-headed Snake **Plate 42**

Unechis gouldii (Gray, 1841)

RANGE: South-western Western Australia.

IDENTIFICATION: Head slightly distinct from the neck; moderately slender body. Dorsal coloration is reddish-brown, with each scale having a fine black edging. The head is black, with paler patches in front of the eye. Labials and ventral surface are whitish.

Mid-body scales are in 15 rows; ventrals number 140 to 177; subcaudals are single, numbering 20 to 38; anal scale is single.

Maximum length is about 600 mm.

REMARKS: This nocturnal species may be found sheltering beneath well-embedded rocks and logs, and often several specimens may be found occupying the same site. Prey consists mostly of small lizards, but smaller snakes are also consumed. Nervous in temperament, this species will bite if provoked. While not considered dangerous, a bite from a large specimen can cause considerable discomfort.

Black-striped Snake **Plate 43**

Unechis nigrostriatus (Krefft, 1864)

RANGE: Coastal north-eastern Australia.

IDENTIFICATION: Head barely distinct from the neck; moderately slender body. Dorsal coloration is pinkish to dark reddish-brown, each scale normally having lighter edging. The top of the head is dark brown to black and a distinct dark vertebral stripe runs from the head to the tip of the tail. Ventral surface is whitish.

Mid-body scales are in 15 rows; ventrals number 160 to 190; subcaudals are single, numbering 45 to 70; anal scale is single.

Maximum length is about 600 mm.

REMARKS: This is a secretive, nocturnal species, about which little is known. It preys upon geckoes and other small lizards. Although venomous, it is not regarded as dangerous to humans.

GENUS *VERMICELLA*

Bandy-bandy **Plate 43**

Vermicella annulata (Gray, 1841)

RANGE: Northern and eastern Australia.

IDENTIFICATION: Head indistinct from the neck; moderately robust body. Coloration is distinctive, being alternate black and white rings.

Mid-body scales are in 15 rows; ventrals number 180 to 320; subcaudals are divided, numbering 12 to 30; anal scale is divided.

Maximum length is about 750 mm.

REMARKS: A nocturnal burrowing species which may be found in a variety of habitats, it is often found under well-embedded rocks, logs, etc. It is an egg-layer and clutches of up to 6 have been recorded; newly hatched young measure about 175 mm in length. Prey consists mostly of Blind Snakes (family: Typhlopidae), but small lizards may also be taken. Inoffensive by nature, it has an unusual defensive display: the body is flattened and elevated in large loops, which are then raised and lowered displaying this snake's striking coloration to advantage. Although venomous, it is not regarded as dangerous to humans.

SUBSPECIES:

Vermicella annulata annulata (Gray, 1841)
Found in eastern and southern Australia, it has a ventral count of 180 to 243.

Vermicella annulata snelli Storr, 1967
Found in north-western, northern and central Australia, it has a ventral count of 254 to 313.

The Dangerous Species

Common Death Adder **Plate 14**

Acanthophis antarcticus (Shaw, 1794)

RANGE: Found through most of far southern Western Australia and South Australia, inland and coastal New South Wales and Queensland to the Barkly Tablelands of the Northern Territory.

IDENTIFICATION: Broad, blunt arrow-shaped head distinct from neck; robust body with a short tapering tail, which terminates in a small curved spine. Coloration is extremely variable, the most common phases being any shade of grey or a russet red, usually with distinct cross-bands. The undersurface is a creamish grey, often with dark blotches.

Mid-body scales may be smooth or weakly keeled, and are in 21 (rarely 23) rows; ventral scales number 110 to 138; subcaudals are mostly single and number 36 to 50; anal plate is single.

Maximum length is about one metre.

REMARKS: Death Adders are a sedentary species, habitually burrowing under soft soil or leaf litter to await passing prey. They are reluctant to move when in repose, relying on their efficient camouflage to render them undetectable. The main danger with this species is the possibility of treading upon, or within striking range, of it, for any movement may provoke a strike. It bears live young and may produce up to 20 young in a litter. Newborn young measure about 140 mm in length. It feeds upon small mammals, birds and reptiles.

Being mainly nocturnal in habit, it is usually encountered on warm nights, when its activity can start at dusk and continue until early morning. Contrary to common belief, the tail tip is not a poisonous "sting", this member being used only to lure prey. Possessing large fangs and a highly potent, neurotoxic venom, the Death Adder is one of our deadliest snakes.

SIMILAR SPECIES: *Acanthophis praelongus*
Virtually indistinguishable to the layman, this is an intermediate form between *antarcticus* and *pyrrhus*. Occurs in northern Australia.

Acanthophis pyrrhus
May be distinguished by its strongly rugose head shields and by normally having more ventral scales (126–160 rather than 110–138).

Denisonia maculata
May be distinguished by having only 17 mid-body scale rows.

Northern Death Adder
Acanthophis praelongus Ramsay, 1877

RANGE: The Kimberleys of Western Australia, northern parts of the Northern Territory and Queensland. Also found in southern New Guinea.

IDENTIFICATION: Broad head distinct from the neck; robust body. Dorsal coloration is extremely variable and may be greyish to dark reddish-brown with numerous darker cross-bands; ventral surface whitish with darker spotting.

Mid-body scales may be smooth to moderately keeled, and are in 21 or 23 rows; ventral scales number 122 to 140; subcaudals are mostly single and number 39 to 57; anal plate is single.

Maximum length is about 800 mm.

REMARKS: As for *Acanthophis antarcticus*.

SIMILAR SPECIES: *Acanthophis antarcticus*

As there is considerable variation in coloration and scalation within both species, they are virtually indistinguishable to the layman.

Acanthophis pyrrhus
Very similar, but may be separated by distribution.

Denisonia maculata
May be distinguished by having only 17 mid-body scale rows.

Desert Death Adder **Plate 15**
Acanthophis pyrrhus Boulenger, 1898

RANGE: Found through arid regions of western and central Australia.

IDENTIFICATION: Broad head distinct from the neck; robust body; thin tail terminating in a spine. Dorsal coloration is brick-red, with numerous dark-edged scales and yellowish cross-bands, which are particularly prominent when the body is distended in anger. Ventral surface is creamish.

Mid-body scales are in 17 to 21 rows and are strongly keeled; ventrals number 126 to 160; subcaudals are usually 50 per cent single and number 42 to 63; anal plate is single.

Maximum length is about 760 mm.

REMARKS: A nocturnal, terrestrial species which spends its days burrowed into loose red sand, especially under clumps of porcupine grass (*Triodia* spp.). It merges so well with this background that it is almost undetectable. It bears live young and produces about 13 young in a litter. Newborn young measure about 160 mm in length. The tail is used as a lure to attract prey, by being placed close to the head and wriggled convulsively if approached by a potential meal. It feeds on small mammals and reptiles. This species is regarded as extremely dangerous.

SIMILAR SPECIES: *Acanthophis praelongus*
The reddish colour phase is virtually indistinguishable to the layman, but may be separated by distribution.

Acanthophis antarcticus
May be distinguished by its smoother head and body scales and by having fewer ventral scales (110–138 rather than 126–160).

Copperhead **Plates 15, 16**

Austrelaps superbus (Günther, 1858)

RANGE: Eastern highlands of New South Wales, through Victoria to the south-eastern corner of South Australia (an isolated population occurs in the Adelaide Hills), also found in Tasmania and Bass Strait islands.

IDENTIFICATION: Head slightly distinct from neck; robust body. Dorsal coloration is extremely variable: New South Wales specimens are predominantly black or tan, while more southern forms may be either black, reddish-brown, copper or brassy. The lower lateral scales are usually much lighter, being either yellow, white or reddish-brown. The undersurface is yellowish or sombre grey.

Mid-body scales are in 15 or 17 rows; ventral scales number 140 to 165; subcaudals are single, numbering 35 to 55; anal plate is single.

Maximum length is about 1.7 metres.

REMARKS: This hardy, diurnal species frequents marshy areas, where it occasionally congregates in large colonies. Favourite haunts are in thick grass tussocks, stone heaps, tree roots and hollow logs. More resistant to cold than any other Australian elapid, it is sometimes observed sun-basking in the freezing conditions of midwinter. It bears live young and may produce about 20 in a litter; newborn young measure about 180 mm in length. It feeds upon frogs, small mammals and reptiles, including its own species.

Quick to retreat when encountered, if provoked it will flatten the neck and body and assume a striking stance. The potent venom is mainly neurotoxic, attacking the muscles of the body and containing some blood-destroying properties. This species is regarded as extremely dangerous.

Bardick

Brachyaspis curta (Schlegel, 1837)

RANGE: From south-western Western Australia, through southern South Australia to western Victoria and south-western New South Wales.

IDENTIFICATION: Broad, depressed head distinct from neck; stout body. Dorsal coloration is variable and may be either grey, olive, brown or brick-red; the lips are usually dotted with white and there may be some pale flecks on the sides. The undersurface is cream to grey.

Mid-body scales are in 19 rows; ventral scales number 130 to 145; subcaudals are single, numbering 30 to 40; anal plate is single.

Maximum length attained is about 0.6 metre.

REMARKS: A small adder-like nocturnal species which prefers the more arid parts of its range, often being found under clumps of porcupine grass (*Triodia* spp.). It bears live young and may produce up to 10 in a litter. It feeds upon frogs, reptiles and small mammals. As this snake has well-developed fangs and a venom which quickly subdues small mammals, a bite may require medical treatment.

Small-eyed Snake **Plate 18**

Cryptophis nigrescens (Günther, 1858)

RANGE: Coastal areas of eastern Australia, from Cape York Peninsula to southern Victoria.

IDENTIFICATION: Head distinct from neck; robust body. Dorsal coloration is uniformly shiny black or grey; ventral surface is white, cream or pink, often with dark blotches.

Mid-body scales are in 15 rows; ventrals number 165 to 210; subcaudals are single, numbering 30 to 46; anal plate is single.

Maximum length is about 1.2 metres.

REMARKS: This nocturnal species occurs in a variety of habitats, but is most prevalent in rocky areas, such as sandstone ridges and other secluded outcrops. In the Blue Mountains, the author and the late L. Robichaux discovered a rock crevice which contained 28 specimens, all entangled into a ball, obviously hibernating. Their sizes ranged from juveniles to large adults. It bears live young and produces up to 5 in a litter; newborn young measure about 110 mm in length. Although regarded in previous years as not dangerous to humans, its potent venom causes muscle damage and has resulted in one adult fatality.

Black Whip Snake **Plate 19**

Demansia atra (Macleay, 1885)

RANGE: Coast and adjacent areas of northern Australia,

from the East Kimberleys of Western Australia through the "Top End" of the Northern Territory to central eastern Queensland. Also found in New Guinea.

IDENTIFICATION: Head deep and narrow, distinct from the neck; long, slender body. Dorsal coloration is black, becoming reddish posteriorly; the head is dark coppery brown without darker spots but dark posterior blotching may be present. The lips, chin, throat and undertail can be pinkish to whitish, while the ventrals are greyish with the anterior ones being edged in black.

Mid-body scales are in 15 rows; ventrals number 176 to 197; subcaudals are divided, numbering 70 to 88; anal scale is divided.

Maximum length is about 1.8 metres.

REMARKS: An extremely active diurnal species, which occasionally becomes semi-nocturnal on warm nights. Considered to be Australia's fastest moving snake, it is nervous and retiring by nature and is disinclined to bite unless provoked. It is an egg-layer and may produce up to 20 eggs in a clutch. It feeds upon small reptiles, frogs, mammals and insects. Although the exact potency of its venom is unknown, bites from large specimens are regarded as potentially dangerous to man.

SIMILAR SPECIES: *Demansia papuensis melaena*
May be distinguished by its higher ventral and subcaudal scale counts, spotted head and its anterior ventrals not being black-edged.

Black Whip Snake (2)
Demansia papuensis melaena Storr, 1978

RANGE: Far northern Australia.

IDENTIFICATION: Head deep and narrow, distinct from the neck; long slender body. Dorsal coloration is black to blackish-brown becoming paler posteriorly; the head is brownish, dotted with darker spots. There is no dark rostral line or comma-like marking around the eye as is present in most other members of the genus. The lips, chin, throat and undertail are white while the remainder of the ventral surface is greyish.

Mid-body scales are in 15 rows; ventral scales number 192 to 220; subcaudals are divided, numbering 78 to 105; anal plate is divided.

Maximum length attained is about 1.8 metres.

REMARKS: This is an active, fast-moving species which although normally diurnal, may be found active on warm nights. It is an egg layer and may produce up to 20 eggs in a clutch. Its main food item is small lizards but it also preys upon other small reptiles, frogs, insects and small mammals. Inoffensive by nature, it is quick to retire if encountered and bites from this species are seldom recorded. It is venomous and because of its large size, bites should be regarded as dangerous.

SIMILAR SPECIES: *Demansia atra*
May be distinguished by its lower ventral and subcaudal counts, its unspotted head and its anterior ventrals being black-edged.

Ornamental Snake **Plate 22**
Denisonia maculata (Steindachner, 1867)

RANGE: Central eastern Queensland

IDENTIFICATION: Broad head distinct from the neck; short robust body. Dorsal coloration is any shade of brown to almost black; the sides are paler with black flecks. The head is speckled with brown and cream and the lips are distinctly barred. Ventral surface is white or cream, with irregular black flecks.

Mid-body scales are in 17 rows; ventrals number 120 to 150; subcaudals are single, numbering 20 to 40; anal scale is single.

Maximum length is about 500 mm.

REMARKS: A nocturnal, terrestrial species which feeds upon frogs and small lizards. It bears live young, producing about 8 in an average litter. If provoked, it becomes very agitated and flattens the entire body, often striking without warning. As its venom is quite potent and produces serious effects in adults, it must be regarded as potentially dangerous to humans.

SIMILAR SPECIES: *Acanthophis antarcticus*
May be distinguished by having 21 or 23 mid-body scale rows.

Pale-headed Snake **Plate 27**
Hoplocephalus bitorquatus (Jan, 1859)

RANGE: Eastern Australia, from about Gosford, New South Wales, to Cape York Peninsula, Queensland.

IDENTIFICATION: Broad head distinct from the neck; moderately robust body. Dorsal coloration is greyish; the head is normally spotted with black and there is a distinct whitish patch on the nape; the lips are barred with black. Ventral surface is cream, often with darker flecks.

Mid-body scales are in 19 or 21 rows; ventral scales are keeled, numbering 190 to 225; subcaudals are single, numbering 40 to 65; anal scale is single.

Maximum length is about 1.2 metres.

REMARKS: This arboreal, nocturnal species favours forested areas, where it shelters under loose bark or in hollow limbs. It bears live young, but the exact number of young is unknown. Large specimens occasionally feed on small mammals, but the major prey item is small lizards. Aggressive, if provoked, it possesses a potent venom which is mainly neurotoxic and bites may require medical treatment.

Broad-headed Snake — Plate 28

Hoplocephalus bungaroides (Boie, 1828)

RANGE: Coastal areas of south-eastern New South Wales.

IDENTIFICATION: Broad head distinct from the neck; moderately robust body. Dorsal coloration is jet black, dotted with numerous yellow scales, which usually form thin irregular cross-bands. Ventral surface is grey to grey-black.

Mid-body scales are in 21 rows; ventral scales are keeled, numbering 200 to 230; subcaudals are single, numbering 40 to 65; anal scale is single.

Maximum length is about one metre.

REMARKS: This colourful arboreal species is mainly nocturnal and frequents secluded sandstone outcrops where it shelters under loose rocks or in crevices. It bears live young and produces up to 8 in a litter. The principal prey item is small lizards, but occasionally frogs and small mammals are taken. If provoked, this aggressive snake stands its ground and, with the neck held in a rigid "S" shape, strikes repeatedly. The potent venom is mainly neurotoxic and bites have caused serious illness in adults.

SIMILAR SPECIES: *Python spilotus spilotus*
The superficial similarity of these two species has already resulted in one fatality (Kinghorn, 1968); they may be readily distinguished by the python's 40 or more mid-body scale rows.

Stephen's Banded Snake **Plates 28, 29**
Hoplocephalus stephensi Krefft, 1869

RANGE: Coastal areas of south-eastern Queensland and northern New South Wales.

IDENTIFICATION: Broad head distinct from the neck; moderately robust body. Dorsal coloration is brown, with broad black cross-bands on the body and tail (occasional unbanded specimens are known). Ventral surface is cream with black blotches.

Mid-body scales are in 21 rows; ventral scales are keeled, numbering 220 to 250; subcaudals are single, numbering 50 to 70; anal plate is single.

Maximum length is about 1.2 metres.

REMARKS: A nocturnal, arboreal species which usually shelters beneath loose bark or in hollow limbs. It produces live young, with one litter of 5 being recorded; newborn young measure about 170 mm in length. It feeds mostly upon small lizards, but it has been recorded taking birds and small mammals. Aggressive, if provoked, its venom is neurotoxic and contains a powerful thrombin, which induces blood clotting. Therefore this species should be considered as potentially dangerous to humans.

Black Tiger Snake **Plates 29, 30**
Notechis ater (Krefft, 1866)

RANGE: Coastal areas and some off-shore islands of South Australia, islands of Bass Strait and Tasmania.

IDENTIFICATION: Head distinct from the neck; robust body. Dorsal coloration is dark brown to jet black, often with obscure cream or yellowish cross-bands. Ventral surface is creamish, yellowish, greyish or dark blue.

Mid-body scales are in 15 to 21 rows; ventrals number 160 to 185; subcaudals are single, numbering 40 to 60; anal scale is single.

Maximum length is about 2.45 metres.

REMARKS: Normally a diurnal, terrestrial species, but may become semi-nocturnal during warm weather. It is found in a variety of habitats, but prefers marshy areas. On the Bass Strait islands, it is usually associated with mutton bird rookeries, sheltering within the burrow complexes and feeding on the newly hatched chicks. Other prey taken includes small mammals, fish, frogs and other reptiles (including its own species). It bears live young and may produce about 20 in a litter; newborn young measure about 270 mm in length. Possessing a potent neurotoxic venom, this snake is one of our most dangerous species.

SUBSPECIES: *Notechis ater ater* (Krefft, 1866)
Found in the Flinders Ranges of South Australia; grows to about one metre.

Notechis ater humphreysi Worrell, 1963
Found in Tasmania and King Island, Bass Strait; grows to about 1.5 metres. Cannibalistic.

Notechis ater niger Kinghorn, 1921
Found on Kangaroo Island, the Sir Joseph Banks

group of islands and adjacent areas of Eyre Peninsula, South Australia; grows to about 1.5 metres.

Notechis ater serventyi Worrell, 1963
Found on Chappell and Badger Islands, of the Furneaux Group, Bass Strait; grows to about 2.45 metres.

Common Tiger Snake **Plate 31**

Notechis scutatus (Peters, 1861)

RANGE: South-eastern Queensland, eastern New South Wales, Victoria, south-eastern South Australia and south-western parts of Western Australia.

IDENTIFICATION: Head slightly distinct from neck; robust body. Dorsal coloration is extremely variable, being olive-grey, green, tan, dark brown or black, with numerous cream or yellow cross-bands. Ventral surface may be yellow, olive-green or grey. It must be noted that unbanded and melanotic specimens also occur.

Mid-body scales are in 15 to 19 rows; ventrals number 140 to 190; subcaudals are single, numbering 35 to 65; anal scale is single.

Maximum length is about two metres.

REMARKS: This species shows a marked preference for well-watered, swampy areas, where it often congregates into large colonies. Normally regarded as a terrestrial diurnal snake, it often displays arboreal habits by climbing trees and shrubs; it also becomes semi-nocturnal in warm weather. It bears live young and may produce more than 40 in a litter; newborn young measure about 150 mm in length. A variety of prey is consumed including frogs, fish, lizards, small mammals and birds. Although preferring to retreat when encountered, if provoked, tiger snakes can become extremely aggressive. The neck and body is flattened, a striking stance is assumed and explosive, warning hisses are emitted. It has a very potent neurotoxic venom, and is regarded as one of our most dangerous snakes.

SUBSPECIES: *Notechis scutatus occidentalis* (Glauert, 1948) Usually black, with or without numerous yellow cross-bands; found in south-western parts of Western Australia.

Notechis scutatus scutatus (Peters, 1861) Found in the south-eastern part of Australia.

Small-scaled Snake or Western Taipan **Plate 32**
Oxyuranus microlepidota (McCoy, 1879)

RANGE: South-western Queensland, extending into north-eastern South Australia, western New South Wales and south-eastern Northern Territory.

IDENTIFICATION: Head indistinct from neck; streamlined body. Dorsal coloration is light to dark brown with numerous dark-edged scales giving a speckled appearance; the head is often glossy black. The undersurface is creamish-yellow with a dark edge on each ventral scale.

Mid-body scales are in 23 or 25 rows; ventral scales number 212 to 237; subcaudals are normally all divided, numbering 54 to 66; anal plate is single.

Maximum length is about 2.7 metres.

REMARKS: A formidable, diurnal species that is normally associated with the flat plains country of south-western Queensland. Shy and retiring, unless provoked, it is quick to retreat into deep earth cracks if disturbed. It is an egg-layer, producing up to 13 in a clutch. It feeds upon small mammals, birds and lizards.

This species is highly venomous and tests conducted by the Commonwealth Serum Laboratories on its neurotoxic venom have shown it to be more potent than that of the Common Brown, Taipan and Tiger Snake. Such potency, combined with its fairly large yield, makes this species not only the most dangerous land snake in Australia but, potentially, the world's most venomous land snake.

SIMILAR SPECIES: *Oxyuranus scutellatus*
May be distinguished by its keeled body scales and its single maxillary tooth.

Pseudonaja nuchalis
May be distinguished by its lower mid-body scale count (17–19 rather than 23).

Taipan

Plate 32

Oxyuranus scutellatus (Peters, 1867)

RANGE: Coastal, eastern Australia from Grafton, New South Wales, to Cape York, then west along the Gulf of Carpentaria. Extends through the top end of the Northern Territory (including Bathurst and Melville Islands) to the Kimberley region of Western Australia.

IDENTIFICATION: Long, deep head distinct from neck; elongate, cylindrical body. Dorsal coloration can be any shade of brown to almost black; the ventral surface is creamish-yellow, with yellow or orange blotches.

Mid-body scales are in 21 or 23 rows (feebly keeled anteriorly); ventral scales number 220 to 250; subcaudals are divided, numbering 45 to 80; anal plate is single.

Maximum length is about three metres.

REMARKS: This species is usually diurnal, being most active in the early morning or late afternoon; however, it may be encountered after dark, especially during extremely hot weather. A favourite retreat is the "wind rows", which border sugar cane paddocks; it also favours rock heaps and ground rubbish, such as sheet iron, timber and fibro. It is an egg-layer and may produce up to 20 in a clutch; newly hatched young measure about 600 mm in length. It feeds upon small mammals, birds and lizards.

The Taipan has an undeserved reputation as being extremely aggressive; actually it is a shy, retiring species which, if given the choice, prefers to retreat rather than attack. If cornered or provoked, however, it will defend itself with a ferocity unequalled by any other Australian snake. Its extreme agility enables it to deliver several lightning-like strikes in rapid succession. This coupled with its large fangs and the quantity of potent neurotoxic venom (which also causes the blood to clot), injected at a bite, make it one of our deadliest species. Close encounters with this dangerous snake should be avoided at all times.

SUBSPECIES: *Oxyuranus scutellatus canni* (Slater, 1956)
A dark form which occurs in New Guinea.

Oxyuranus scutellatus scutellatus (Peters, 1867)
Found in northern and north-eastern Australia.

SIMILAR SPECIES: *Oxyuranus microlepidota*
May be distinguished by its smooth body scales and by its more numerous maxillary teeth.

Mulga or King Brown Snake

Plate 33

Pseudechis australis (Gray, 1842)

RANGE: Australia generally, with the exception of eastern New South Wales, most of Victoria, the south-east corner of South Australia and the extreme south of Western Australia.

IDENTIFICATION: Head slightly distinct from neck; long robust body. Dorsal coloration is variable, being any shade of brown to almost black; each scale is tipped with red or black, giving some specimens a distinct reticulated pattern. Ventral surface is creamish-yellow.

Mid-body scales are in 17 rows; ventrals number 185 to 225; subcaudals are usually 50 per cent divided and number 50 to 75; anal scale is divided.

Maximum length is about 2.75 metres.

REMARKS: Though often encountered during the day, this large, formidable species is mainly nocturnal. It is wide-ranging, being found in a variety of habitats. Usually regarded as a species that bears live young, this has been thrown into some doubt recently, when a captive female laid 16 eggs, which hatched after 70 days' incubation. The newly hatched young measured about 250 mm in length. It feeds upon small mammals, birds and reptiles, being prone to cannibalism. As very large specimens have few natural enemies, they are often unperturbed by man's presence and are reluctant to move away when encountered. Aggressive if provoked, it will flatten the neck and body and prepare to strike. Because of its large size and the quantity of venom injected at a bite, it is regarded as extremely dangerous to humans.

Collett's Snake
Pseudechis colletti Boulenger, 1902

RANGE: Central, western Queensland.

IDENTIFICATION: Head slightly distinct from neck; robust body. Dorsal coloration is variable, the typical form being chocolate brown to black above, with the lower sides pink or cream, these two colours meeting in irregular cross-bands or variegations. The undersurface is creamish-yellow to orange.

Mid-body scales are in 19 rows; ventral scales number 215 to 235; subcaudals number 50 to 70; usually about 25 per cent are divided; anal plate is divided.

Maximum length is about 1.8 metres.

REMARKS: This uncommon, diurnal species is the most colourful member of its genus. It lays eggs, producing up to 13 in a clutch; the hatchlings measure about 370 mm in length. It feeds upon small mammals, birds, reptiles and amphibians.

Normally a placid snake, it becomes nervous if provoked and will flatten the entire body in a threat display. Its venom is very similar to that of the Mulga Snake *Pseudechis australis* and it may be regarded as dangerous to humans.

SIMILAR SPECIES: *Pseudechis guttatus*
May be distinguished by having less than 210 ventral scales.

Blue-bellied or Spotted Black Snake **Plate 33**
Pseudechis guttatus De Vis, 1905

RANGE: South-eastern Queensland to north-eastern New South Wales.

IDENTIFICATION: Head indistinct from neck; robust body. Dorsal coloration is normally black, with or without some scales spotted with cream. The undersurface is blue-grey, often with cream blotches. A light colour form is occasionally encountered; this is cream above, speckled with black-edged scales.

Mid-body scales are in 19 rows; ventral scales number 175 to 205; subcaudals number 45 to 65, usually some anterior scales are single, the rest are divided; anal plate is divided.

Maximum length is about 1.8 metres.

REMARKS: This species favours dry inland areas, but also frequents river floodplains and coastal forest. Though mainly diurnal, it often becomes semi-nocturnal during warm weather. There is some controversy over its mode of reproduction; it has been recorded as bearing live young as well as being an egg-layer. Charles, Whitaker and Shine (1979) record three instances of egg-laying, with the largest clutch numbering 13 eggs. Incubation required 11 to 12 weeks and hatchlings measured about 280 mm in length. It feeds upon small mammals, frogs and reptiles.

It is typically nervous and shy but if provoked it will flatten the neck and body and hiss loudly. Its venom is the most toxic of the genus *Pseudechis*, commonly causing intense local pain and tenderness of the lymph nodes. This species must be regarded as dangerous to humans.

SIMILAR SPECIES: *Pseudechis colletti*
May be distinguished by having more than 210 ventral scales.

Red-bellied Black Snake **Plate 34**
Pseudechis porphyriacus (Shaw, 1794)

RANGE: Eastern Australia, from the Atherton Tablelands, Queensland, through New South Wales and

Victoria to south-eastern South Australia.

IDENTIFICATION: Head slightly distinct from neck; robust body. Dorsal coloration is glossy black, with the lower sides bright red, orange or pink, to almost white. The undersurface is red or pink (rarely white) edged with black, underside of tail black.

Mid-body scales are in 17 rows; ventral scales number 180 to 210; subcaudals number 40 to 65, usually some anterior scales are single, the rest are divided; anal plate is divided.

Maximum length is about 2.1 metres.

REMARKS: This diurnal species frequents well-watered areas such as swamps, banks of rivers, creeks and lakes. It bears live young and may produce up to 20 in a litter; the newborn young measure about 200 mm in length. A voracious feeder, it preys upon frogs, fish, birds, reptiles and small mammals.

Habitually shy and quick to retreat when encountered, if provoked it will assume a striking stance, flatten the neck and body and hiss loudly, in a display that is mostly bluff. The venom is the least toxic of the genus *Pseudechis* but is known to affect the body muscles and may cause paralysis. Even though fatalities are rare, this species should be considered as dangerous to humans.

Dugite

Plate 34

Pseudonaja affinis Günther, 1872

RANGE: South-western corner of Western Australia, then east along a narrow coastal strip to the South Australian border.

IDENTIFICATION: Small head indistinct from neck; slender, streamlined body. Dorsal coloration is usually dark brown, olive or grey, speckled irregularly with black scales. The undersurface can be off-white to creamish-yellow.

Mid-body scales are in 19 rows; ventral scales number 190 to 230; subcaudals are divided, numbering 50 to 70; anal plate is divided.

Maximum length is about 1.85 metres.

REMARKS: An alert, fast-moving, diurnal snake which, although found through a wide variety of habitats, shows a marked preference for sandy localities. It is an egg-layer and may produce up to 20 eggs in a clutch; hatchlings measure about 180 mm in length. It feeds upon small mammals, birds, reptiles and amphibians.

The Dugite possesses a potent venom and is very aggressive if provoked. It is one of our more deadly species. Its venom is mainly neurotoxic but also contains severe blood-destroying properties which can cause massive haemorrhage.

SUBSPECIES: *Pseudonaja affinis affinis* (Günther, 1872) Found through the majority of the species range, it grows to about 1.85 metres.

Pseudonaja affinis tanneri (Worrell, 1961) Restricted to islands of the Recherche Archipelago, south-west Western Australia; grows to about one metre.

Speckled Brown Snake **Plate 35**

Pseudonaja guttata (Parker, 1926)

RANGE: Central Queensland, extending into eastern areas of the Northern Territory.

IDENTIFICATION: Depressed head, slightly distinct from neck; moderate, streamlined body. Dorsal coloration is variable, the typical form being beige to light brown with numerous black-edged scales. A banded form is also common, with 9 to 18 dark cross-bands evenly spaced from the nape to the tail. The undersurface is creamish-yellow with orange blotches.

Mid-body scales are in 19 or 21 rows; ventral scales number 190 to 220; subcaudals are divided, numbering 45 to 70; anal plate is divided.

Maximum length is about 1.2 metres.

REMARKS: This diurnal species is a specialised black-soil plains dweller and shelters in deep earth cracks, especially those in the near vicinity of water. It is an egg-layer, but virtually nothing is known of clutch sizes. It feeds upon frogs, small mammals and reptiles.

Although a placid snake, in comparison to other members of the genus, the toxicity of its venom is unknown and it should be regarded as dangerous.

Ingram's Brown Snake **Plate 35**
Pseudonaja ingrami (Boulenger, 1908)

RANGE: The Barkly Tableland of the Northern Territory, to adjacent areas of western Queensland.

IDENTIFICATION: Head slightly distinct from neck; body slightly more robust than other members of the genus. Dorsal coloration is variable, the typical forms being either entirely chocolate brown, or reddish-brown with yellow centres to the body scales. A yellowish-brown form with dark edging on the body scales and a dark brown head and nape is also common. The undersurface is yellow with two series of orange blotches, which are more prominent anteriorly.

Mid-body scales are in 17 rows; ventral scales number 190 to 223; subcaudals are divided, numbering 55 to 72; anal plate is divided.

Maximum length is about 1.8 metres.

REMARKS: This diurnal snake is a specialised black-soil plains dweller, preferring areas of thick Mitchell grass where it shelters down deep earth cracks. It is an egg-layer, with one clutch of 12 eggs being recorded. It feeds upon small mammals and reptiles.

Although not normally aggressive, due to its size and the unknown potency of its venom it must be regarded as extremely dangerous.

SIMILAR SPECIES: *Pseudonaja textilis textilis*
May be distinguished by having a pinkish coloured mouth, rather than blackish, and by having fewer infralabial scales (6 rather than 7).

Ringed Brown Snake **Plate 36**
Pseudonaja modesta Günther, 1872

RANGE: Arid regions of all mainland states, with the exception of Victoria.

IDENTIFICATION: Head barely distinct from neck; slender, streamlined body. Dorsal coloration is olive, tan or rich reddish-brown, with a series of four to twelve narrow black cross-bands evenly spaced along the body. The top of the head and a broad band on the nape are dark brown to black; these markings, along with the body cross-bands, may be indistinct or completely absent in aged specimens. The undersurface is cream to pale yellow, often with orange or grey blotches.

Mid-body scales are in 17 rows; ventral scales number 145 to 175; subcaudals are divided, numbering 35 to 55; anal plate is divided.

Maximum length is about 60 centimetres.

REMARKS: This, the smallest member of the brown snake genus, is mainly diurnal but becomes semi-nocturnal during warm weather. Favoured habitats are low rock outcrops and dry water-courses, where it shelters under debris and down abandoned animal burrows. It is an egg-layer and may produce up to 11 in a clutch.

Although not regarded as dangerous to humans, care should be taken with large specimens.

Western Brown Snake **Plate 36**
Pseudonaja nuchalis Günther, 1858

RANGE: Australia generally, with the exception of the eastern coastal strip, south-eastern Victoria and the extreme south and south-west corner of Western Australia.

IDENTIFICATION: Small head, indistinct from neck; slender, streamlined body. Dorsal coloration is extremely variable, the predominant form being olive-grey or any shade of brown (sometimes merging on black), with scattered dark scales on the neck. Other forms may be strongly banded, or have a glossy black head and nape. The undersurface is creamish-yellow with a dual series of reddish or grey blotches.

Mid-body scales are in 17 (rarely 19) rows; ventral scales number 180 to 230; subcaudals are divided, numbering 50 to 70; anal plate is divided.

Maximum length is about 1.5 metres.

REMARKS: This common, swift-moving species is mainly diurnal, but in northern parts of its range becomes largely nocturnal during warm weather. It is an egg-layer and may produce up to 22 in a clutch; hatchlings measure about 220 mm in length. It preys upon lizards, frogs and small mammals.

Although usually less aggressive than the

common brown snake, its venom is also powerfully neurotoxic, with some blood destroying properties, and it can be regarded as one of our deadliest species.

SIMILAR SPECIES: *Oxyuranus microlepidota*
May be distinguished by its higher mid-body scale count (23 rather than 17–19).

Common Brown Snake **Plate 37**
Pseudonaja textilis (Duméril, Bibron & Duméril, 1854)

RANGE: Found through Queensland, New South Wales and Victoria, to south-eastern South Australia. Isolated populations occur in three areas of the Northern Territory — Macdonnell Ranges, Barkly Tablelands and the Victoria River Downs/Wave Hill district, to the north-east corner of Western Australia.

IDENTIFICATION: Head indistinct from neck; body slender and streamlined. Dorsal coloration is variable, being any shade of grey or brown, sometimes merging on black. Ventral surface may be cream, yellow or brown, heavily splotched with brown or grey. Juveniles may be strongly banded, the bands usually fading with maturity.

Mid-body scales are in 17 rows; ventrals number 185 to 235; subcaudals are divided, numbering 45 to 75; anal scale is divided.

Maximum length is about 2.5 metres.

REMARKS: This fast-moving, terrestrial species may be found in a variety of habitats, but usually prefers drier areas. Normally diurnal, it is an egg-layer and may produce up to 30 eggs in a clutch; incubation requires about 11 weeks and hatchlings measure about 270 mm in length. A voracious feeder, it preys upon small mammals, birds, reptiles and amphibians. Extremely aggressive, if provoked, it will pugnaciously press home an attack. A characteristic striking stance is assumed by holding the forebody high in an "S" shape. It will then, with jaws agape, strike repeatedly. Although its fangs and venom yield are small, the venom is highly neurotoxic and coagulant, with some blood-destroying properties, making it one of our most dangerous and deadly species.

SUBSPECIES: *Pseudonaja textilis inframacula* (Waite, 1925)
Found on Eyre and Yorke Peninsulas, South Australia. Dorsal coloration is dark brown, usually with numerous irregular, darker scales, ventral surface is brown, splotched with grey. It grows to about 1.5 metres.

Pseudonaja textilis textilis (Duméril, Bibron & Duméril, 1854)
Found through the rest of the species range.

SIMILAR SPECIES: *Pseudonaja ingrami*
May be distinguished by having a blackish coloured mouth, rather than pinkish, and by having more infralabial scales (7 rather than 6).

Curl or Myall Snake **Plate 40**
Suta suta (Peters, 1863)

RANGE: Most of South Australia, New South Wales, Queensland and the Northern Territory, extending into eastern Western Australia. Also found in the north-west corner of Victoria.

IDENTIFICATION: Depressed head distinct from neck; robust body. Dorsal coloration may be any shade of brown (occasionally olive-green), often with dark tips on the scales, giving a reticulated appearance. The head and nape are dark brown to black and a dark line, bordered by white scales, extends from below the eyes to the snout. These markings are barely discernible or completely absent in aged specimens. The undersurface is white or cream.

Mid-body scales are in 19 or 21 rows; ventral scales number 150 to 170; subcaudals are single, numbering 20 to 35; anal plate is single.

Maximum length is about 0.9 metre.

REMARKS: This nocturnal, terrestrial species ranges through a wide variety of habitats but is most common in dry, arid areas. It shelters down earth cracks or under logs and other ground debris. It bears live young and may produce about 6 in a litter. It feeds upon lizards, frogs and small mammals. Of unpredictable nature, this snake derives its most popular vernacular name from its threat display, which consists of flattening the body, curling tightly, then lashing from side to side. Although not previously regarded as dangerous, the toxicity of its mainly neurotoxic venom (Worrell) is not fully known and bites from large specimens may require medical treatment.

Rough-scaled Snake

Plate 41

Tropidechis carinatus (Krefft, 1863)

RANGE: Two isolated coastal populations occur, one in north-eastern Queensland, the other from south-eastern Queensland to about Barrington Tops, New South Wales.

IDENTIFICATION: Head distinct from neck; robust body. Dorsal coloration is olive-green to dark brown, usually with narrow, dark cross-bands. Ventral surface is creamy-yellow or olive-green, with darker splotches.

Body scales are strongly keeled and are in 23 rows at mid-body; ventrals number 160 to 185; subcaudals are single, numbering 50 to 60; anal scale is single.

Maximum length is about one metre.

REMARKS: This species favours rainforest, or areas adjacent to water. Mainly diurnal in habit, it becomes semi-nocturnal during warm weather. It bears live young but little is known of litter sizes. It feeds upon small mammals, reptiles and amphibians. Normally inoffensive, it is, however, very aggressive when provoked and will bite at every opportunity. The venom is mainly neurotoxic, but also affects the blood and causes severe muscle damage. This snake must be regarded as extremely dangerous to man.

SIMILAR SPECIES: *Amphiesma mairii*

This harmless species is superficially very similar but may be distinguished by having fewer mid-body scale rows (15–17 rather than 23).

FAMILY HYDROPHIIDAE

Sea Snakes **Plates 44, 45**
Hydrophiidae

These specially adapted marine snakes are closely related to our venomous land snakes. They may be distinguished by valvular nostrils, high on the snout, and a vertically compressed, paddle-shaped tail, which is used for swimming. All sea snakes are front fanged and highly venomous. They are mostly confined to the warmer waters of the tropics, but occasionally have been found as far south as Tasmania. There is considerable diversity in shape, colour and size amongst the 32 species recorded from Australian seas. Sizes range from small slender forms fully grown at 0.5 metre to large, robust species reaching up to 2.7 metres.

Temperament varies with individual specimens but all species will bite if hurt or provoked. Professional fishermen run the greatest risk of being bitten when removing snakes that have been accidentally netted. To employees on prawning trawlers, sea snakes are part of nearly every catch, and considering that innumerable specimens are handled (either killed or thrown overboard), the percentage of bites is minimal. A combination of *Enhydrina schistosa* (Beaked Sea Snake) and Tiger Snake antivenoms effectively neutralises the venoms of our known deadly species.

Bibliography

BOULENGER, G. A. (1961), *Catalogue of Snakes in British Museum,* reprint, New York.

COGGER, H. G. (1967), *Australian Reptiles in Colour,* A. H. & A. W. Reed, Sydney.

COGGER, H. G. (1979), *Reptiles and Amphibians of Australia,* revised edition, A. H. & A. W. Reed, Sydney.

COGGER, H. G. (1980), *Snakes,* Longman Cheshire, Melbourne.

COVACEVICH, J. (1970), *The Snakes of Brisbane,* revised edition, Queensland Museum, Brisbane.

GARNET, J. R. (1968), *Venomous Australian Animals Dangerous to Man,* Commonwealth Serum Laboratories, Parkville.

GLAUERT, L. (1950), *A Handbook of the Snakes of Western Australia,* West Australian Naturalist, Perth.

GOW, G. F. (1977), "A New Species of Python from Arnhem Land", *Australian Zoologist* 19 (2): pp. 133–9.

GOW, G. F. (1977), *Snakes of the Darwin Area,* Museums and Art Galleries of the Northern Territory, Darwin.

GOW, G. F. (1981), "A New Species of Python from Central Australia", *Australian Journal of Herpetology,* Vol.1, No.1.

GOW, G. F. (1977), "Darwin's Colubrid Snakes", *Australian Natural History Magazine,* Australian Museum, Sydney.

GOW, G. F. (1980), "Notes on the Desert Death Adder *Acanthophis pyrrhus,* Boulenger 1898 with the first reproductive record", *Northern Territory Naturalist,* Vol.1, No.3.

GOW, G. F. (1980) "Notes on the Taipan *Oxyuranus scutellatus* with two new distribution records", *Northern Territory Naturalist,* Vol.1, No.3.

KINGHORN, J. R. (1956), *The Snakes of Australia,* 2nd Edition. Angus & Robertson, Sydney.

KREFFT, G. (1869), *Snakes of Australia,* Australian Museum, Sydney.

LOVERIDGE, A. (1945), *Reptiles of the Pacific World,* Macmillan, New York.

McPHEE, D. R. (1979), *The Observer's Book of Snakes and Lizards of Australia,* Methuen Australia, Sydney.

SLATER, K. R. (1956), *A Guide to the Dangerous Snakes of Papua,* Government Printer, Port Moresby.

WAITE, E. R. (1898), *Australian Snakes,* Thomas Shine, Sydney.

WAITE, E. R. (1929), *Reptiles and Amphibians of South Australia,* South Australian Museum, Adelaide.

WORRELL, E. (1966), *Dangerous Snakes of Australia and New Guinea,* Angus & Robertson, Sydney.

WORRELL, E. (1963), *Reptiles of Australia,* Angus & Robertson, Sydney.

Index

Numbers in bold type are colour plate references

The Plates

Plate 1

Top: BLIND SNAKE, *Ramphotyphlops nigrescens*
Bottom: BLACK-HEADED PYTHON, *Aspidites melanocephalus*

Plate 2

WOMA, *Aspidites ramsayi*

Plate 3

Top: GREEN PYTHON, *Chondropython viridis*
Bottom: GREEN PYTHON, *Chondropython viridis*
Juvenile colour change

Plate 4

Top: CHILDREN'S PYTHON, *Liasis childreni*
Bottom: WATER PYTHON, *Liasis mackloti*
Photo — the author

Plate 5

Top: OLIVE PYTHON, *Liasis olivaceus*
Photo — P. Horner
Bottom: SCRUB PYTHON, *Python amethistinus*

Plate 6

CENTRALIAN CARPET PYTHON, *Python bredli*
Photo—the author

Plate 7

Top: OENPELLI PYTHON, *Python oenpelliensis*
Photo — the author
Bottom: DIAMOND PYTHON, *Python spilotus spilotus*

Plate 8

Top: CARPET PYTHON, *Python spilotus variegatus*
Bottom: LITTLE FILE SNAKE, *Acrochordus granulatus*
Photo — P. Horner

Plate 9

Top: JAVAN FILE SNAKE, *Acrochordus javanicus*
Bottom: BROWN TREE SNAKE, *Boiga irregularis*
Photo—the author

Plate 10

Top: FRESHWATER SNAKE OR KEELBACK, *Amphiesma mairii*

Bottom: COMMON TREE SNAKE, *Dendrelaphis punctulatus*

Plate 11

Top: COMMON TREE SNAKE, *Dendrelaphis punctulatus*
Golden colour phase from coastal Northern Territory
Bottom: SLATY-GREY SNAKE, *Stegonotus cucullatus*

Plate 12

Top: BOCKADAM, *Cerberus australis*
Photo—the author

Bottom: *Cerberus rhynchops novaeguineae*

Plate 13

Top: MACLEAY'S WATER SNAKE, *Enhydris macleayi*
Bottom: WHITE-BELLIED MANGROVE SNAKE, *Fordonia leucobalia*

Plate 14

Top: COMMON DEATH ADDER, *Acanthophis antarcticus*
Grey colour phase

Bottom: COMMON DEATH ADDER, *Acanthophis antarcticus*
Red colour phase

Plate 15

Top: DESERT DEATH ADDER, *Acanthophis pyrrhus*
Bottom: COPPERHEAD, *Austrelaps superbus*

Plate 16

Top: COPPERHEAD, *Austrelaps superbus*
Orange colour phase
Bottom: WHITE-CROWNED SNAKE, *Cacophis harrietae*

Plate 17

Top: DWARF CROWNED SNAKE, *Cacophis krefftii*
Bottom: GOLDEN-CROWNED SNAKE, *Cacophis squamulosus*

Plate 18

Top: SMALL-EYED SNAKE, *Cryptophis nigrescens*
Bottom: SECRETIVE SNAKE, *Cryptophis pallidiceps*

Plate 19

Top: BLACK WHIP SNAKE, *Demansia atra*
Photo—J. Cann
Bottom: MARBLE-HEADED WHIP SNAKE, *Demansia olivacea*

Plate 20

Top: YELLOW-FACED WHIP SNAKE, *Demansia psammophis*
Bottom: *Demansia reticulata*

Plate 21

Top: COLLARED WHIP SNAKE, *Demansia torquata*
Bottom: DE VIS' BANDED SNAKE, *Denisonia devisii*

Plate 22

Top: ORNAMENTAL SNAKE, *Denisonia maculata*
Photo — J. Cann
Bottom: LITTLE SPOTTED SNAKE, *Denisonia punctata*

Plate 23

Top: CROWNED SNAKE OR WERR, *Drysdalia coronata*
Bottom: WHITE-LIPPED SNAKE, *Drysdalia coronoides*

Plate 24

Top: *Drysdalia rhodogaster*
Bottom: RED-NAPED SNAKE, *Furina diadema*

Plate 25

Top: DUNMALL'S SNAKE, *Glyphodon dunmalli*
Bottom: BROWN-HEADED SNAKE, *Glyphodon tristis*

Plate 26

Top: GREY SNAKE, *Hemiaspis damelii*
Bottom: MARSH SNAKE, *Hemiaspis signata*

Plate 27

Top: MARSH SNAKE, *Hemiaspis signata*
Dark colour phase from coastal southern Queensland
Bottom: PALE-HEADED SNAKE, *Hoplocephalus bitorquatus*

Plate 28

Top: BROAD-HEADED SNAKE, *Hoplocephalus bungaroides*
Bottom: STEPHEN'S BANDED SNAKE, *Hoplocephalus stephensi*

Plate 29

Top: STEPHEN'S BANDED SNAKE, *Hoplocephalus stephensi*
Unbanded phase

Bottom: KING ISLAND TIGER SNAKE, *Notechis ater humphreysi*
Photo—J. Cann

Plate 30

PENINSULA TIGER SNAKE, *Notechis ater niger*

Plate 31

Top: COMMON TIGER SNAKE, *Notechis scutatus scutatus*
Bottom: WESTERN TIGER SNAKE, *Notechis scutatus occidentalis*

Plate 32

Top: SMALL-SCALED SNAKE OR WESTERN TAIPAN,
Oxyuranus microlepidota
Photo — the author

Bottom: TAIPAN, *Oxyuranus scutellatus scutellatus*

Plate 33

Top: MULGA OR KING BROWN SNAKE, *Pseudechis australis*
Bottom: BLUE-BELLIED OR SPOTTED BLACK SNAKE, *Pseudechis guttatus*

Plate 34

Top: RED-BELLIED BLACK SNAKE, *Pseudechis porphyriacus*
Bottom: DUGITE, *Pseudonaja affinis affinis*

Plate 35

Top: SPECKLED BROWN SNAKE, *Pseudonaja guttata*
Bottom: INGRAM'S BROWN SNAKE, *Pseudonaja ingrami*
Photo — P. Horner

Plate 36

Top: RINGED BROWN SNAKE, *Pseudonaja modesta*
Bottom: WESTERN BROWN SNAKE, *Pseudonaja nuchalis*

Plate 37

Top: COMMON BROWN SNAKE, *Pseudonaja textilis textilis*
Bottom: COMMON BROWN SNAKE, *Pseudonaja textilis textilis*
From some areas juveniles may be strongly banded

Plate 38

Top: AUSTRALIAN CORAL SNAKE, *Simoselaps australis*
Bottom: DESERT BANDED SNAKE, *Simoselaps bertholdi*
Photo — the author

Plate 39

Top: NARROW-BANDED BURROWING SNAKE, *Simoselaps fasciolatus*
Bottom: HALF-GIRDLED SNAKE, *Simoselaps semifasciatus*

Plate 40

Top: *Simoselaps? warro*
Bottom: CURL OR MYALL SNAKE, *Suta suta*

Plate 41

Top: ROUGH-SCALED SNAKE, *Tropidechis carinatus*
Bottom: CARPENTARIA SNAKE, *Unechis carpentariae*

Plate 42

Top: LITTLE WHIP SNAKE, *Unechis flagellum*
Bottom: BLACK-HEADED SNAKE, *Unechis gouldii*

Plate 43

Top: BLACK-STRIPED SNAKE, *Unechis nigrostriatus*
Bottom: BANDY-BANDY, *Vermicella annulata*

Plate 44

ELEGANT SEA SNAKE, *Hydrophis elegans*
Photo — the author

Plate 45

YELLOW-BELLIED SEA SNAKE, *Pelamis platurus*

Plate 46

Plate 47

Aquarium set up

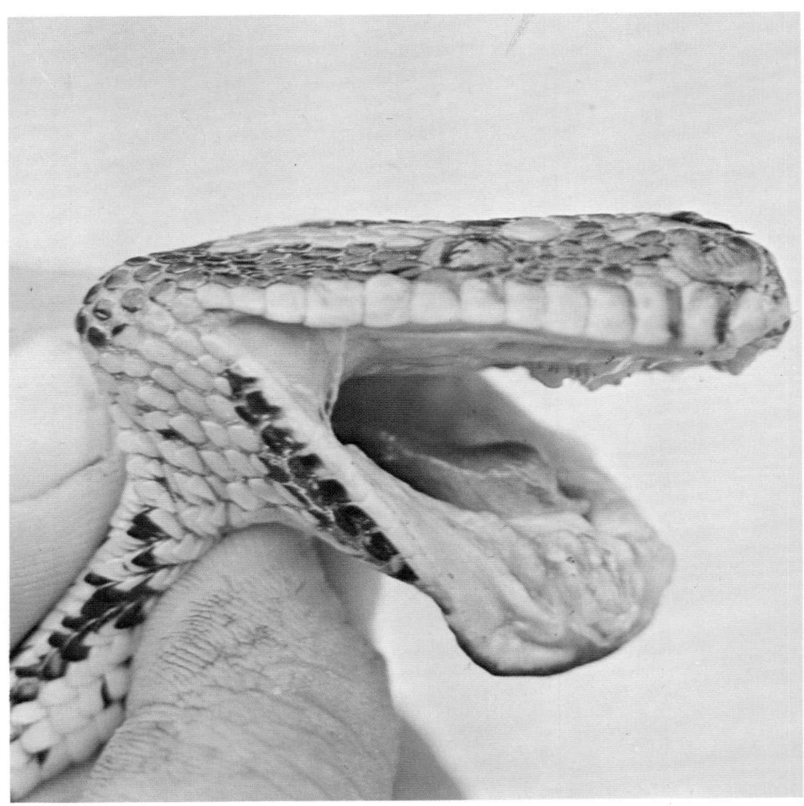

Plate 48

Canker